# NES®

# Middle Grades General Science Practice Questions

I0880197



Mometrix

TEST PREPARATION

# Dear Future Exam Success Story

First of all, **THANK YOU** for purchasing Mometrix study materials!

Second, congratulations! You are one of the few determined test-takers who are committed to doing whatever it takes to excel on your exam. **You have come to the right place.** We developed these practice tests with one goal in mind: to deliver you the best possible approximation of the questions you will see on test day.

Standardized testing is one of the biggest obstacles on your road to success, which only increases the importance of doing well in the high-pressure, high-stakes environment of test day. Your results on this test could have a significant impact on your future, and these practice tests will give you the repetitions you need to build your familiarity and confidence with the test content and format to help you achieve your full potential on test day.

**Your success is our success**

**We would love to hear from you!** If you would like to share the story of your exam success or if you have any questions or comments in regard to our products, please contact us at **800-673-8175** or **support@mometrix.com**.

Thanks again for your business and we wish you continued success!

Sincerely,
The Mometrix Test Preparation Team


Printed in the United States of America

# Table of Contents

# Practice Test #1

**1. Which of the following does NOT display an appropriate or safe use of chemicals?**

a. Never taste any chemicals.
b. To test odors, waft the odors towards your nose with a cupped hand.
c. Never return unused chemicals to the stock bottle.
d. When diluting acids, always pour the water into the acid.

**2. Which of the following wastes may be suitable for sink or sewer disposal?**

a. Acetic acid
b. Benzene
c. Acetone
d. Mercury

**3. Which of the following describes the correct short-term storage method for liquid-filled pH probes?**

a. Store the pH probes in distilled water.
b. Store the pH probes on a dry shelf.
c. Store the pH probes in a potassium chloride solution.
d. Store the pH probes in hydrochloric acid.

**4. When lighting a Bunsen burner, the flame is luminous yellow. Which of the following procedures is the correct way to properly adjust this flame?**

a. Decrease the air supply.
b. Increase the air supply.
c. Decrease the gas supply.
d. Increase the gas supply.

**5. When using a microscope, which objective provides the greatest field of view?**

a. 4X
b. 10X
c. 40X
d. 100X

**6. When working with chemicals in a laboratory, which of the following describes the use of appropriate apparel?**

a. Always wear gloves and aprons or lab coats. Wear goggles when needed.
b. Always wear goggles and aprons or lab coats. Wear gloves when needed.
c. Always wear goggles and gloves. Wear aprons or lab coats when needed.
d. Always wear aprons or lab coats. Wear gloves and goggles when needed.

**7. When working in the laboratory, what is the minimum length of time an eye should be flushed if a chemical gets in the eye?**

a. 2 minutes
b. 10 minutes
c. 15 minutes
d. 30 minutes

**8. According to the laboratory safety rules, what should students be instructed to do first in case of a laboratory fire?**

a. Notify the instructor
b. Locate the nearest exit
c. Use the fire extinguisher
d. Open the windows

**9. Which of the following ideas most aligns with Darwin's work in *On the Origin of Species*?**

a. If an organism changes during its life in order to adapt to its environment, those changes are passed on to its offspring.
b. The geological processes that alter the earth are uniform through time.
c. Human populations will rapidly increase unless kept in check by limits in food supply.
d. Nature selects the best-adapted varieties to survive and reproduce.

**10. Which of the following historical figures is NOT correctly matched with his contribution to modern science?**

a. Louis Pasteur and the germ concept of disease
b. Thomas Edison and the theory of relativity
c. Johannes Kepler and the laws of planetary motion
d. Nicolaus Copernicus and the heliocentric view of the solar system

**11. Which of the atomic models listed below is the most recent?**

a. Rutherford's atomic model
b. Bohr's atomic model
c. Thomson's atomic model
d. Dalton's atomic model

**12. Which of the following is NOT a statement of one of the laws established by Isaac Newton?**

a. The lateral pressure exerted by a moving fluid decreases as the fluid's speed increases.
b. For every action there is an opposite and equal reaction.
c. The acceleration of an object is directly related to the force applied to the object and inversely related to the object's mass.
d. The attraction between two objects is directly related to the masses of the objects and inversely related to the square of the distance between the two objects.

**13. Which of the following is NOT supported by Dalton's atomic theory of matter?**

a. Differences in properties of elements are due to differences in the atoms of the elements.
b. Atoms of a particular element all have the same properties, such as size and mass.
c. Every element consists of tiny particles called atoms, which can be split into even smaller pieces.
d. Chemical processes result from the rearrangement, combination, and separation of atoms.

**14. Who proposed the quantum theory of light?**

a. James Maxwell
b. Christiaan Huygens
c. Isaac Newton
d. Albert Einstein

**15. Which of the following statements is NOT congruent with the theory of plate tectonics?**

a. The continents were once connected in the large supercontinent Pangea.
b. The tectonic plates are part of the Earth's lithosphere.
c. Seafloor spreading is evidence of tectonic plate movement.
d. Subduction occurs at divergent boundaries.

**16. The best way to separate isotopes of the same element is to exploit:**

a. Differences in chemical reactivity
b. Differences in reduction potential
c. Differences in toxicity
d. Differences in mass

**17. Nuclear chain reactions, such as the kind that is exploited in nuclear power plants, are propagated by what subatomic particle(s)?**

a. Protons
b. Neutrons
c. Electrons
d. Neutrons and protons

**18. Which of the following statements about radioactive decay is true?**

a. The sum of the mass of the daughter particles is less than that of the parent nucleus.
b. The sum of the mass of the daughter particles is greater than that of the parent nucleus.
c. The sum of the mass of the daughter particles is equal to that of the parent nucleus.
d. The sum of the mass of the daughter particles cannot be accurately measured.

**19. An alpha particle consists of:**

a. Two electrons and two protons
b. Two electrons and two neutrons
c. Four neutrons
d. Two protons and two neutrons

**20. When a solid is heated and transforms directly into the gaseous phases, this process is called:**

a. Sublimation
b. Fusion
c. Diffusion
d. Condensation

**21. Place the following elements in order of decreasing electronegativity:**

N, As, Bi, P, Sb

a. As > Bi > N > P > Sb
b. N > P > As > Sb > Bi
c. Bi > Sb > As > P > N
d. P > N > As > Sb > Bi

**22. Arrange the following compounds from most polar to least polar:**

$F_2$, $CH_3CH_2Cl$, $NaCl$, $CH_3OH$

a. $NaCl > CH_3OH > CH_3CH_2Cl > F_2$
b. $F_2 > NaCl > CH_3OH > CH_3CH_2Cl$
c. $CH_3OH > NaCl > F_2 > CH_3CH_2Cl$
d. $NaCl > F_2 > CH_3OH > CH_3CH_2Cl$

**23. Adding a catalyst to a reaction will do which of the following?**

a. Shift the reaction equilibrium towards the products
b. Increase the temperature of the reaction
c. Decrease the energy of activation for the reaction
d. Increase the purity of the reaction products

**24. Place the following in the correct order of increasing acidity:**

$H_3PO_4$, $HF$, $HCl$, $H_2O$, $NH_3$

a. $H_3PO_4 < H_2O < NH_3 < HF < HCl$
b. $NH_3 < H_2O < HF < H_3PO_4 < HCl$
c. $H_2O < NH_3 < HF < H_3PO_4 < HCl$
d. $NH_3 < H_2O < HF < HCl < H_3PO_4$

**25. Three 1-kg blocks—one made of iron, one of lead, one of nickel—are heated from 20 °C to 30 °C. Which of the following statements about the blocks is true?**

a. The lead heats faster than the iron and the nickel.
b. The iron requires more heat to reach 30 °C than the nickel or lead.
c. All three blocks require a different amount of heat to reach 30 °C.
d. The iron requires more time to reach 30 °C than the nickel or the lead.

**26. In the reaction $Pb + H_2SO_4 \rightarrow PbSO_4 + H_2$:**

a. Lead is reduced, and hydrogen is oxidized.
b. Lead is oxidized, and hydrogen is oxidized.
c. Lead is reduced, and sulfate is oxidized.
d. Lead is oxidized, and hydrogen is reduced.

**27. Proteins are made up of repeating subunits of which of the following?**

a. Sugars
b. Triglycerides
c. Amino acids
d. Nucleic acids

**28. The density of a material refers to:**

a. Mass per volume
b. Mass per mole
c. Molecular weight per volume
d. Moles per volume

**29. Which of the following types of chemicals are considered generally unsafe to store together?**

I. Liquids and solids
II. Acids and bases
III. Reducing agents and oxidizing agents
IV. Metals and salts

a. I, II
b. II, III
c. III, IV
d. I, IV

**30. Methylmercury is a toxin produced indirectly from what energy source?**

a. Oil
b. Natural gas
c. Wood
d. Coal

**31. The masses of four different objects, taken with different scales, were 23.04 g, 7.12 g, 0.0088 g, and 5.423 g. What is the total mass of all four objects to the proper number of decimal places?**

a. 35.59180 g
b. 35.5918 g
c. 35.60 g
d. 35.59 g

**32. Which of the following is a vector quantity?**

a. Distance
b. Speed
c. Velocity
d. Time

**33. A person walks 4 meters in a single direction. He then changes directions and walks an additional 9 meters. What is the total magnitude of the displacement of the person?**

a. It is 13 meters.
b. It is always larger than 9 meters but less than 13 meters.
c. It is less than 13 meters and as small as 5 meters.
d. It is less than 5 meters.

**34. Consider the two vectors below:**

Vector A: 

Vector B: 

**Which vector best represents the vector obtained by subtracting $A$ from $B$ $(\vec{B} - \vec{A})$?**

a. 

b. 

c. 

d. 

**35. An automobile increased its speed uniformly from 20 m/s to 30 m/s at a rate of 5 $m/s^2$. During this time, it traveled 50 meters. How long did it take the automobile to make this change?**

a. 5 seconds
b. 2 seconds
c. 10 seconds
d. 20 seconds

**36. You throw a baseball straight up near the surface of Earth and it falls back to the ground. Which statement is true about the acceleration of the baseball at the top of its path? (Ignore air resistance.)**

a. The acceleration is zero.
b. The acceleration changes sign.
c. The acceleration is $-9.8\ m/s^2$.
d. The acceleration continues to increase.

**37. Which of the following demonstrations best illustrates Newton's first law?**

a. Giving a small push to a billiard ball that was at rest on a smooth, level table and letting it roll on the table
b. Dragging a box on a table at a constant speed by exerting just enough force to overcome the force of friction
c. Trying without success to move a heavy bureau or filing cabinet on the floor
d. Running a current through two parallel wires

**38. Consider the following statements about Newton's law:**

I. A newton is a fundamental unit.
II. Mass and acceleration are inversely related when the force is constant.
III. Newton's first law can be derived from Newton's second law.
IV. Newton's second law can be derived from the universal law of gravity.

**Which of the statements are true?**

a. I, II, and III.
b. II and III only.
c. III only.
d. None of them

**39. A box with a weight of 10 newtons is resting on a table, which is resting on the ground. In the context of Newton's third law, if we consider the force of the box on the table to be the action force, which of the following statements is true?**

a. The force of the table on the box is the reaction force.
b. The force of the table on the ground is the reaction force.
c. The force of the ground on the table is the reaction force.
d. There is no reaction force because the system is in equilibrium.

**40. A lead sphere 10 centimeters in diameter is attached to a 10-meter wire and suspended from a beam in a large warehouse. A lead sphere 1 meter in diameter is hung next to the smaller sphere, almost touching. Ignoring friction, which statement is true?**

a. The small sphere will move slightly toward the big sphere, but the big sphere will not move.
b. The big sphere will move slightly toward the small sphere, but the small sphere will not move.
c. Neither sphere will move.
d. Both spheres will move slightly toward each other.

**41. A 10-kg plastic block is at rest on a flat wooden surface. The coefficient of static friction between wood and plastic is 0.6, and the coefficient of kinetic friction is 0.5. How much horizontal force is needed to start the plastic box moving?**

a. 5 N
b. 49 N
c. 59 N
d. 98 N

**42. The pulley in the device below has no mass and is frictionless. The larger mass is 30 kg, and the smaller mass is 20 kg. What is the acceleration of the masses?**

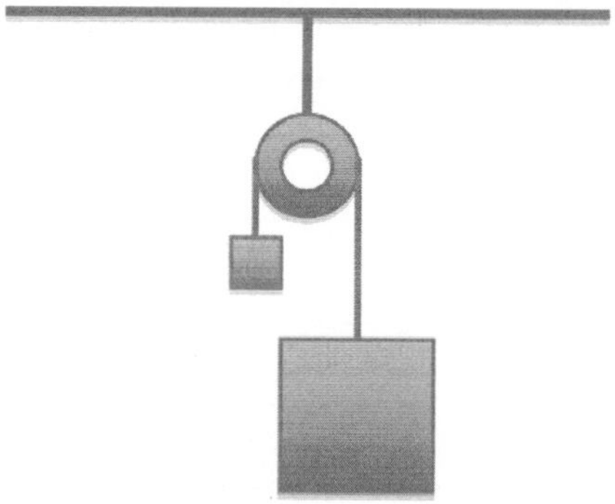

a. $0.5\ m/s^2$
b. $2.0\ m/s^2$
c. $9.8\ m/s^2$
d. $98\ m/s^2$

**43. A force of 25.0 N pulls three blocks connected by a string on a frictionless surface. What is the tension in the rope between the 4.0-kg block and the 2.0-kg block?**

a. 0 N
b. 11.1 N
c. 16.7 N
d. 25 N

**44. You blow up a rubber balloon and hold the opening tight with your fingers. You then release your fingers, causing air to blow out of the balloon. This pushes the balloon forward, causing the balloon to shoot across the room. Which of Newton's laws best explains the cause of this motion?**

a. Newton's First Law
b. Newton's Second Law
c. Newton's Third Law
d. Newton's Fourth Law

**45. Which has a greater moment of inertia about an axis through its center: a solid cylinder or a hollow cylinder? Both cylinders have the same mass and radius.**

a. Solid cylinder
b. Hollow cylinder
c. Both have the same moment of inertia.
d. It depends on how quickly the cylinders are rolling.

**46. Two cars driving in opposite directions collide. If you ignore friction and any other outside interactions, which of the following statements is always true?**

a. The total momentum is conserved.
b. The sum of the potential and kinetic energy is conserved.
c. The total velocity of the cars is conserved.
d. The total impulse is conserved.

**47. Suppose a moving railroad car collides with an identical stationary car and the two cars latch together. Ignoring friction, and assuming no deformation on impact, which of the following statements is true?**

a. The speed of the first car decreases by half.
b. The collision is elastic.
c. The speed of the first car is doubled.
d. There is no determining the final speed because the collision was inelastic.

**48. A 4-kilogram bowling ball moving at 10 meters per second hits a stationary 1-kilogram bowling ball in a head-on elastic collision. What is the speed of the stationary ball after the collision?**

a. 0 m/s
b. 10 m/s
c. Less than 10 m/s, but not 0 m/s
d. More than 10 m/s

**49. A teacher pulls a box across the floor at a uniform speed. He pulls it with a spring scale showing that the force of kinetic friction is 2 newtons. How much total work is done in moving the box 5 meters?**

a. 0 joules
b. 0.4 joules
c. 10 joules
d. 20 joules

**50. Which statement best explains why the work done by a gravitational force on an object does not depend on the path the object takes?**

a. Work depends on the path when there is friction. The longer the path, the more energy is required to overcome friction.
b. Gravitational fields that arise from the interaction between point masses always produce elliptical paths of motion.
c. Because gravitational force is conservative, the work it does depends only on the change in gravitational potential energy, which depends only on the initial and final heights
d. When an object falls down, the work done by gravity is positive, and when an object is thrown up, the work done by gravity is negative.

**51. Which statement correctly states the work-energy theorem?**

a. The change in kinetic energy of an object is equal to the work done by the object.
b. The change in kinetic energy of an object is equal to the work done on an object.
c. The change in potential energy of an object is equal to the work done by the object.
d. The change in potential energy of an object is equal to the work done on an object.

**52. An athlete's foot is in contact with a kicked football for 100 milliseconds and exerts a force on the football over a distance of 20 centimeters. The force starts at 0 N and increases linearly to 2,000 N for 50 milliseconds through a distance of 10 centimeters and then decreases linearly for 50 milliseconds through a distance of 10 centimeters. What is the average power of the athlete's foot while it is in contact with the ball?**

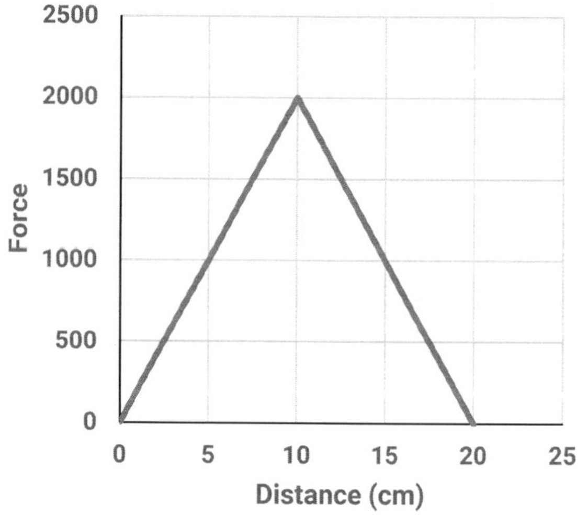


a. 2 kilowatts
b. 4 kilowatts
c. 2,000 kilowatts
d. 4,000 kilowatts

**53. A motorcycle weighs twice as much as a bicycle and is moving twice as fast. Which of the following statements is true?**

a. The motorcycle has four times as much kinetic energy as the bicycle.
b. The motorcycle has eight times as much kinetic energy as the bicycle.
c. The bicycle and the motorcycle have the same kinetic energy.
d. The bicycle has four times as much kinetic energy as the motorcycle.

**54. Which of the following statements about energy is false?**

a. Mechanical energy is always conserved in an isolated system.
b. Total energy is always conserved in an isolated system.
c. Energy is never created or destroyed.
d. Matter can be transformed into energy

**55. Conservative forces are forces that do not lose energy to processes like friction and radiation and where the total mechanical energy is conserved. Which statement best explains why the work done by a conservative force on an object does not depend on the path the object takes?**

a. This is the definition of a conservative force.
b. The work done by the force of friction on an object depends on the distance the object moves.
c. Work can be positive, negative, or zero.
d. If a force is conservative, any component of the force is equal to the change in potential energy divided by the change in position.

**56. How much does it cost to operate a 5-kilowatt electric motor for 12 hours if electricity is 6 cents per kilowatt-hour?**

a. \$0.025
b. \$3.60
c. \$14.40
d. \$360

**57. Which of the following statements best explains what is meant by the phase of a wave?**

a. The height of a wave in $2\pi$ radians.
b. The length of a wave in $2\pi$ radians.
c. The period of oscillation of a wave.
d. An angle indicating the wave cycle's instantaneous location.

**58. A 100-kg bungee jumper jumps off a bridge, attached to a 20-meter bungee cord. After bouncing around for a minute he finally comes to rest. The stretched cord is now 25 meters long. What is the spring constant of the bungee cord?**

a. 20 newtons per meter
b. 39 newtons per meter
c. 49 newtons per meter
d. 196 newtons per meter

**59. What is the speed of a wave with a frequency of 12 Hz and a wavelength of 3 meters?**

a. 12 meters per second
b. 36 meters per second
c. 4 meters per second
d. 0.25 meters per second

**60. Two waves, each of which has an amplitude of *A*, cross paths. At the point where they cross, the peak of one wave meets the trough of another wave. What is the resulting displacement of the medium at the point where the waves cross?**

a. 0
b. $A$
c. $2A$
d. $-A$

**61. In resonance, small vibrations can produce a larger standing wave that becomes stronger than the original vibrations, assuming the vibrations are at the right frequency to generate resonance. If a pendulum is vibrated at a resonance frequency, what would you expect to happen?**

a. The period of the pendulum will increase.
b. The time between swings will decrease.
c. The pendulum will swing higher.
d. The length of the pendulum will decrease.

**62. Transverse traveling waves propagate through a taut string of length 20 meters at a speed of 4 m/s. Standing waves are set up in this string which is fixed at both ends. What is the smallest frequency possible for the standing waves?**

a. 0.1 Hz
b. 0.05 Hz
c. 0.2 Hz
d. 0.4 Hz

**63. Which of the following statements about refraction is true?**

a. Refraction means a change in the direction of the wave.
b. The angle of reflection equals the angle of refraction.
c. The frequency in a refracted wave changes.
d. The phase of a refracted wave changes.

**64. What corresponds to the amplitude of a sound wave?**

a. Loudness
b. Pressure differential of fluctuations
c. Magnitude of motion of air molecules
d. Power

**65. The density of helium is much lower than that of air. How does the speed of sound traveling through helium gas compare to the speed of sound in air?**

a. It is faster.
b. It is slower.
c. It is the same speed.
d. It cannot be determined without knowing their atomic masses.

**66. What property of a sound corresponds to the frequency of the sound wave in air?**

a. Pitch
b. High and low
c. Timbre
d. Overtones

**67. Which of the following could be an end product of transcription?**

a. rRNA
b. DNA
c. Protein
d. snRNP

**68. All of the following are common ways of controlling eukaryotic gene expression EXCEPT:**

a. Regulatory proteins
b. Nucleosome packing
c. Methylation of DNA
d. Operons

**69. Transfer of DNA between bacteria using a narrow tube called a pilus is known as:**

a. Transformation
b. Transduction
c. Operation
d. Conjugation

**70. A virus that has been incorporated into the DNA of its host is called a:**

a. Lysogenic cycle
b. Lytic cycle
c. Retrovirus
d. Provirus

**71. A virus is actively replicating DNA in what stage?**

a. Lysogenic cycle
b. Lytic cycle
c. Retrovirus
d. Provirus

**72. A bacterial mini-chromosome used in recombinant DNA technology is called a**

a. Centromere
b. Telomere
c. Plasmid
d. Transposon

**73. Which of the following parts of an angiosperm gives rise to the fruit?**

a. Pedicel
b. Filament
c. Sepal
d. Ovary

**74. Which of the following structures is NOT present in gymnosperms?**

a. Leaves
b. Pollen
c. Flowers
d. Stomata

**75. Which of the following plant structures allows for gas exchange?**

a. Xylem
b. Phloem
c. Cuticle
d. Stomata

*Refer to the following for questions 76–77:*

*Diagram representing a cross section of a tree trunk:*

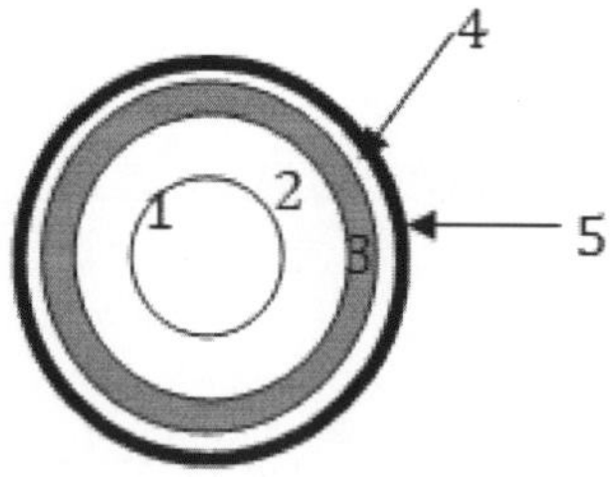


**76. Which structure contains tissue that is dead at maturity?**

a. 1
b. 2
c. 3
d. 4

**77. Which structure transports carbohydrates to the roots?**

a. 1
b. 2
c. 3
d. 4

**78. In ferns, the joining of egg and sperm produces a zygote, which will grow into the:**

a. Gametophyte
b. Sporophyte
c. Spore
d. Sporangium

**79. Which of the following is an example of the alternation of generations life cycle?**

a. Asexual reproduction of strawberries by runners
b. Annual plants that live through a single growing season
c. Ferns that have a large diploid and a diminutive haploid stage
d. Insects that have distinct larval and adult stages

*Refer to the following for questions 80–81:*

*Diagram of a complete, perfect flower*

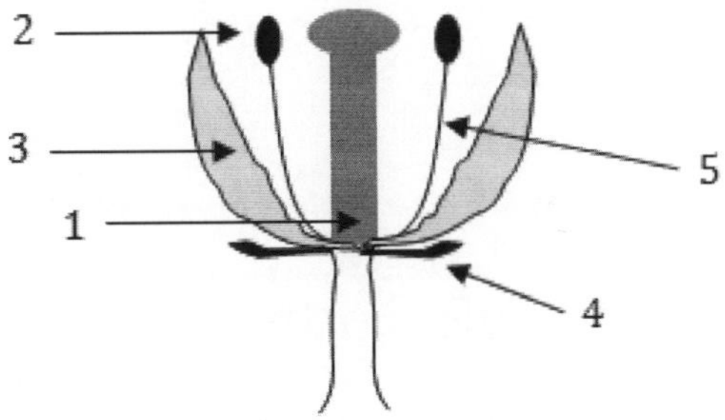


**80. The structure in which microspores are produced is:**

a. 1
b. 2
c. 3
d. 4

**81. The structures composed solely of diploid cells are:**

a. 1, 2, and 3
b. 2, 3, and 4
c. 3, 4, and 5
d. 1, 4, and 5

**82. Which of the following plant hormones is most likely to delay aging when sprayed on cut flowers and fruit?**

a. Ethylene
b. Gibberellins
c. Cytokinins
d. Abscisic acid

**83. Which of the following would most likely be disruptive to the flowering time of a day-neutral plant?**

a. Daylight interrupted by a brief dark period
b. Daylight interrupted by a long dark period
c. High daytime temperatures
d. Night interrupted by a brief exposure to red light

**84. Animals exchange gases with the environment in all of the following ways EXCEPT**

a. Direct exchange through the skin
b. Exchange through gills
c. Exchange through stomata
d. Exchange through tracheae

**85. Which of the following blood components is involved in blood clotting?**

a. Red blood cells
b. Platelets
c. Plasma proteins
d. Leukocytes

**86. Which section of the digestive system is responsible for water reabsorption without producing digestive enzymes?**

a. The large intestine
b. The duodenum
c. The small intestine
d. The gallbladder

**87. Which of the following processes is an example of positive feedback?**

a. High $CO_2$ blood levels stimulate respiration which decreases blood $CO_2$ levels
b. High blood glucose levels stimulate insulin release, which makes muscle and liver cells take in glucose
c. Increased nursing stimulates increased milk production in mammary glands
d. Low blood oxygen levels stimulate erythropoietin production which increases red blood cell production by bone marrow

**88. Which hormone is NOT secreted by the placenta throughout pregnancy?**

a. Human chorionic gonadotropin (hCG)
b. Gonadotropin-releasing hormone (GnRH)
c. Estrogen
d. Progesterone

**89. Polar bodies are a by-product of:**

a. Meiosis I
b. Meiosis II
c. Both meiosis I and II
d. Zygote formation

**90. In which of the following stages of embryo development are the three primary germ layers first present?**

a. Zygote
b. Gastrula
c. Morula
d. Blastula
e. Coelomate

**91. Which of the following extraembryonic membranes is an important source of nutrition in many nonhuman animal species but NOT in humans?**

a. Amnion
b. Allantois
c. Yolk sac
d. Chorion

**92. Which of the following is NOT a mechanism that contributes to cell differentiation and development in embryos?**

a. Asymmetrical cell division
b. Asymmetrical cytoplasm distribution
c. Organizer cells
d. Location of cells on the lineage map

**93. Which of the following is true of the gastrula?**

a. It is a solid ball of cells.
b. It has three germ layers.
c. It is an extraembryonic membrane.
d. It gives rise to the blastula.

**94. Minerals that form on the sea floor from discarded shells are most likely part of which chemical class?**

a. Sulfate
b. Organic
c. Carbonate
d. Silicate

**95. The lithification process results in the formation of which of the following types of rocks?**

a. Sedimentary
b. Intrusive igneous
c. Extrusive igneous
d. Metamorphic

**96. Which of the following types of rock solidifies deepest beneath the Earth's surface?**

a. Hypabyssal
b. Plutonic
c. Volcanic
d. Detrital

**97. Which of the following factors directly contributes to soil erosion?**

a. Air pollution from cars and factories
b. Use of pesticides
c. Deforestation and overgrazing
d. Water pollution caused by excess sedimentation

**98. Physical weathering of rocks can be caused by all of the following EXCEPT:**

a. The freezing and thawing of water on the surface of rocks
b. Changes in temperature
c. Oxidation
d. Changes in pressure due to the removal of overlying rocks

**99. Which of the following is NOT an example of chemical weathering of rocks?**

a. Highly acidic rainwater causes dissolution of rocks.
b. Anhydrous minerals in rocks absorb water, causing them to enlarge and create fractures within the rocks.
c. Salt water penetrates fractures in rocks and leaves behind salt crystals that cause fractures.
d. Iron atoms in rocks react with atmospheric oxygen, which causes oxidation.

**100. Which of the following statements is true of minerals (such as olivine) that are found at the top of Bowen's reaction series?**

a. They are classified as metamorphic.
b. They weather more quickly than rocks found lower in the series.
c. They crystallize at lower temperatures than rocks found at the bottom of the series.
d. They can only be made artificially.

**101. Metamorphic rock is produced when which of the following undergoes profound changes as a result of exposure to intense pressure and heat?**

a. A batholith
b. A protolith
c. An igneous rock
d. A sedimentary rock

**102. All of the following are examples of metamorphic rocks EXCEPT:**

a. Granite
b. Quartzite
c. Slate
d. Marble

**103. When metamorphic rock is stressed unevenly during recrystallization, it can result in:**

a. Foliation
b. Contact metamorphism
c. Regional metamorphism
d. Extrusion

**104. When two tectonic plates are moving laterally in opposing directions, this is called a(n):**

a. Transform boundary
b. Compressional boundary
c. Oppositional boundary
d. Lateral boundary

**105. Which of the following statements correctly describes a difference between the lithosphere and the asthenosphere?**

a. The asthenosphere is composed of atmospheric gas, while the lithosphere is composed of liquids and solids.
b. The asthenosphere is hotter and more fluid than the lithosphere.
c. The lithosphere is hotter and has a different chemical composition than the asthenosphere.
d. Heat is transferred through conduction in the asthenosphere, while it is transferred through convection in the lithosphere.

**106. The most recently formed parts of the Earth's crust can be found at:**

a. Subduction zones
b. Compressional boundaries
c. Extensional boundaries
d. Mid-ocean ridges

*Refer to the following for question 107:*

After a laboratory experiment that involved using various chemical solutions, you and your lab partner are asked to clean up your workspace. The teacher states that any chemicals that have been poured into a new container should be disposed of, but the chemicals still in their original bottles can be placed into storage.

**107. Which of the following is NOT a recommended storage practice for laboratory chemicals?**

a. Chemicals should be stored at the appropriate temperature and humidity.
b. Chemicals should be dated when received and when opened.
c. Chemicals may be routinely stored on bench tops.
d. Chemicals should be stored on shelves with raised outer edges.

**108. Which of the following events directly results in a volcanic eruption?**

a. A batholith forms beneath the Earth's surface.
b. Magma fills vertical and horizontal fractures in the Earth's crust, creating sills and dikes.
c. An oceanic plate is subducted by a continental plate.
d. A dike reaches the Earth's surface, and a plume passes through it.

**109. Which of the following is true of a volcano that is thought to be dormant?**

a. It will probably never erupt again, and it is quite safe for people to live near its base.
b. It is expected to erupt some time again in the future, but danger is not imminent.
c. It is expected to erupt soon, and evacuation should be commenced.
d. It is a shield volcano that is erupting, but people living near the volcano should not expect their lives to be significantly disrupted.

**110. The Earth's magnetic field protects it from:**

a. Excess heat from the Sun
b. Radio waves from black holes
c. Solar wind
d. Impacts from space debris

**111. In 1912, Alfred Wegener proposed a theory often referred to as "the Pangaea Theory." This theory was based on which of the following ideas?**

a. The Earth's magnetic poles have reversed several times throughout history.
b. Tectonic plates move because of convection currents in the mantle.
c. Mountains are formed by tectonic plates pushing against one another.
d. The continents once formed a single land mass, but they have since drifted apart.

**112. The process that causes lithospheric plates to move over the surface of the mantle is called:**

a. Conduction
b. Convection
c. Tension
d. Subduction

**113. Which of the following statements correctly describes the relationship between temperature and density in water?**

a. As the temperature of liquid water decreases, density decreases monotonically.
b. As the temperature of frozen water (ice) increases, density increases monotonically.
c. Water in the solid state generally has a higher density than water in the liquid state.
d. Water in the liquid state generally has a higher density than water in the solid state.

**114. Ammonia has a specific heat capacity greater than that of water. This means that:**

a. Water vaporizes at a higher temperature than ammonia.
b. It takes more energy to increase the temperature of ammonia than it does to increase the temperature of water.
c. Water is always denser than ammonia.
d. Water is only denser than ammonia at higher temperatures.

**115. What is the point of a phase diagram where a substance can exist as a solid, a liquid, and a gas?**

a. Isothermal point
b. Isobaric point
c. Triple point
d. Critical point

*Refer to the following for question 116:*

> The planet's oceans are experiencing climate changes, pollution, and overfishing. In some areas, zones that would normally host abundant aquatic life are now considered "dead zones."

**116. The main human-caused reason for these "dead zones" is:**

a. Evaporation
b. Invasive species
c. Use of chemical fertilizers
d. Global warming

**117. The majority of the solar energy that reaches Earth is absorbed by:**

a. Glaciers
b. Landmasses
c. Oceans
d. The Earth's atmosphere

**118. The majority of weather phenomena occur in which part of the Earth's atmosphere?**

a. Troposphere
b. Stratosphere
c. Hydrosphere
d. Ionosphere

**119. A guyot is defined as:**

a. Any undersea mountain more than 1,000 meters high
b. A seamount with a flattened top
c. An undersea mountain chain
d. A trough in the ocean floor

**120. Approximately 96.5% of seawater is composed of:**

a. Hydrogen and sodium
b. Hydrogen and oxygen
c. Oxygen and sodium
d. Chlorine and sodium

**121. Which of the following is NOT an impact of strip mining of coal?**

a. Destruction of landscapes, forest, and wildlife habitats
b. Dust and noise pollution
c. Chemical contamination of groundwater
d. Lowering of the water table

**122. Which of the following is NOT an effect on the environment due to deforestation?**

a. Loss of biodiversity
b. Soil erosion
c. Decrease in carbon dioxide in atmosphere
d. Disruptions in the water cycle

**123. Which of the following is NOT true about land reclamation?**

a. Land for agricultural use may be reclaimed by draining submerged wetlands.
b. Land reclamation may destroy habitats and increase biodiversity.
c. Land reclamation creates new lands from ocean beds, riverbeds, or lakebeds.
d. Land reclamation may result in soil liquefaction during earthquakes.

**124. Which of the following is a disadvantage of biomass energy?**

a. Using it releases a lot of carbon.
b. It is non-renewable.
c. It requires a lot of space.
d. Current processes require rare earth metals to utilize the energy.

**125. Which of the following is a disadvantage of fossil fuels?**

a. Extraction processes are extremely dangerous.
b. There is no way to control pollution from their processing.
c. They are difficult to store safely.
d. Their use contributes to global warming.

**126. Which of the following is a description of buckminsterfullerene?**

a. A one-atom-thick sheet of carbon
b. A carbon molecule $C_{60}$ that forms a hollow sphere
c. A long hollow tube of carbon atoms
d. A particle between 1 and 100 nanometers in size

**127. Which of the following is currently the greatest benefit of genetically modified crops?**

a. Increased profits for farmers
b. Increased nutrition for consumers
c. Increased shelf life of foods
d. Decreased allergens for consumers

**128. DNA electrophoresis accomplishes which of the following?**

a. Breaking DNA into fragments
b. Separating DNA fragments by size
c. Extracting DNA from evidence
d. Identifying key genetic codes with radioactive markers

**129. Which of the following is NOT a natural process that purifies water?**

a. Filtration
b. Photosynthesis
c. Evaporation
d. Bacterial action

**130. Which of the following is NOT a true statement about how batteries work?**

a. A battery works by completing a circuit within an electrical device.
b. Batteries store energy in the form of chemical energy.
c. The cathode is the reducing agent.
d. Electrons are lost at the anode.

**131. Which of the following is NOT a characteristic of laser light from a particular source?**

a. Laser light is of one wavelength.
b. Laser light is coherent.
c. Laser light is of one frequency.
d. Laser light is multidirectional.

**132. Which of the following is the mathematical principle used to calculate a user's position based on information from the GPS satellites in the user's area?**

a. Triangulation
b. Trilateration
c. Quadlateration
d. Quadangulation

**133. Which of the following common household products is NOT correctly matched with the chemical associated with it?**

a. Vinegar and acetic acid
b. Glass cleaner and sodium hypochlorite
c. Baking soda and sodium bicarbonate
d. Rubbing alcohol and isopropanol

**134. Which of the following household products is NOT correctly matched with the formula of the chemical it's associated with?**

a. Salt, NaCl
b. Sugar, $C_{12}H_{22}O_{11}$
c. Hydrogen peroxide, $H_2O_2$
d. Chalk, $NaCO_3$

**135. Which of the following is NOT a benefit of biodegradable plastic?**

a. Biodegradable plastics reduce the volume of trash in landfills.
b. Biodegradable plastics help conserve petroleum supplies.
c. Biodegradable plastics are cheaper to produce than alternatives.
d. Biodegradable plastics lower the amount of energy used in production.

# Answer Key and Explanations for Test #1

**1. D:** When diluting acids, the acid should always be added to the water. This way, if splashing occurs, only water is splashed out of the beaker. Additionally, this procedure ensures that only a small amount of acid is present in a much larger volume of water. This is especially important when diluting sulfuric acid, because large amounts of heat may be released in the hydration process, which could cause a small amount of water to boil rapidly.

**2. A:** If diluted, acetic acid may be disposed of by sink or sewer. Vinegar is a 5% acetic acid solution and is commonly used in the kitchen. In general, alkanoic acids with 5 or fewer carbon atoms, such as acetic acid, butyric acid, and formic acid, may be disposed of by sink or sewer. Chemicals such as benzene, acetone, and mercury should never be disposed of by sink or sewer.

**3. C:** The pH probes should be stored according to the manufacturer's instructions. In general, pH probes should never be stored in water or stored dry without first draining the electrode. They should always be stored in an appropriate buffer or reference electrolyte, which is usually a 3M – 4M potassium chloride solution.

**4. B:** A properly adjusted flame should be nearly colorless or blue with an inner and outer cone. If the flame is yellow, increase the air supply. If the flame burns noisily, reduce the gas supply.

**5. A:** The field of view is the diameter of the circle of light that is seen when one looks into the microscope. As the power of the objective increases, the field of view gets smaller. Therefore, the objective with the greatest field of view is the one with the lowest power.

**6. B:** Teachers and students should always wear goggles and aprons or lab coats when working with chemicals, including cleanup. Gloves should be worn as needed.

**7. C:** Eyewash stations should be capable of delivered rinsing fluid to both eyes for a minimum of 15 minutes. The stations should be located in an accessible area where a person can reach the station in no more than 10 seconds.

**8. A:** Appropriate laboratory safety rules should include instructions to always notify the instructor in case of any emergency. In the case of a fire, the instructor should be notified first. Then appropriate measures can be taken to actually put out the fire.

**9. D:** Darwin introduced his idea of natural selection in *On the Origin of Species*, in which he stated that nature selects the best-adapted varieties to survive and reproduce. Lamarck wrote *Philosophie Zoologique*, in which he proposed a theory of inheritance of acquired characteristics. This theory states that if an organism changes during its life to adapt to its environment, those changes are passed on to its offspring. Lyell wrote *Principles of Geology*, in which he introduced his idea of uniformitarianism, which states that the geological processes that alter the earth are uniform through time. Malthus wrote *An Essay on the Principle of Population*, in which he stated that human populations will rapidly increase unless kept in check by limits in food supply.

**10. B:** Albert Einstein is known for both the special theory of relativity and the general theory of relativity. Thomas Edison was an inventor best known for inventing the light bulb and phonograph.

**11. B:** Dalton stated that atoms are hard spheres. Thomson proposed the plum pudding model, in which electrons are embedded in a sphere of positive charge. Rutherford introduced the planetary model, in which electrons circularly orbit a small central nucleus. Bohr's model stated that electrons move in regions of space called orbits. This would later be expanded to "orbitals" of the later quantum-mechanical model.

**12. A:** Bernoulli's principle states that the lateral pressure exerted by a moving fluid decreases as the fluid's speed increases. This principle is named after Daniel Bernoulli.

**13. C:** John Dalton proposed the atomic theory of matter in 1803. He stated that each element consists of tiny, indivisible particles called atoms. He did not believe that an atom could be further broken down.

**14. D:** Isaac Newton proposed the particle or corpuscular theory of light. Huygens proposed the wave theory of light. Maxwell showed that light can be modeled as an electromagnetic wave. Einstein described electromagnetic radiation as bundles of energy proportional to frequency in the quantum theory of light.

**15. D:** Subduction occurs at convergent boundaries. Subduction is the process that occurs when two tectonic plates collide and one plate moves under the other plate.

**16. D:** Isotopes of the same element must have the same chemical behavior, and (A), (B), and (C) all represent, in one form or another, chemical behavior. Isotopes differ in mass, and this can be used to separate them by some appropriate physical property.

**17. B:** In a nuclear chain reaction, free neutrons released from nuclear fission cause a nucleus to split and release more neutrons.

**18. A:** Radioactive decay converts mass into energy ($E = mc^2$). The mass of products is always less than that of the starting materials since some mass is now energy.

**19. D:** An alpha particle is a helium nucleus, which contains two protons and two neutrons.

**20. A:** Sublimation is the process of a solid changing directly into a gas without entering the liquid phase. Fusion refers to melting a solid into a liquid. Diffusion is the process of a material dispersing throughout another. Condensation is generally a gas turning into a liquid.

**21. B:** The trend within any column of the periodic table is that electronegativity decreases going down the column.

**22. A:** NaCl is an ionic salt, which is the most polar. $F_2$ is nonpolar since the two atoms share the electrons in an equal and symmetrical manner. $CH_3OH$ is an alcohol with a very polar O-H bond. $CH_3CH_2Cl$ is also a polar molecule due to the unequal sharing of electrons in the C-Cl bond.

**23. C:** Catalysts lower the energy barrier between products and reactants and thus increase the reaction rate. Catalysts do not change the thermodynamic position of equilibrium, reaction temperature, or product purity on their own.

**24. B:** $NH_3$ is ammonia, which is a base. $H_2O$ is amphoteric, meaning that it can act as either a weak acid or a weak base. HF is actually a weak acid, despite fluorine being the most electronegative atom. The small size of the F results in a stronger bond between the H and F, which reduces acidity since this bond will be harder to break. $H_3PO_4$, phosphoric acid, is high in acidity and HCl is a very strong acid, meaning it completely dissociates.

**25. C:** Because all unique materials have differing heat capacities, no two can heat up the same way. All require different amounts of heat to warm to the same temperature.

**26. D:** Lead (Pb) goes from a 0 oxidation state to a 2+ oxidation state and is therefore oxidized. Oxidation is the loss of electrons. Hydrogen goes from a 1+ oxidation state to a 0 oxidation state and is therefore reduced. Reduction is the gaining of electrons.

**27. C:** Proteins are large polypeptides, composed of many amino acids linked together by an amide bond. DNA and RNA are nucleic acids made up of repeating nucleotides. Carbohydrates are long chains of sugars. Triglycerides are fats and are composed of a glycerol molecule and three fatty acids.

**28. A:** Density is mass per volume, typically expressed in units such as $g/cm^3$, or $kg/m^3$.

**29. B:** Acids and bases will react violently if accidentally mixed, as will reducing and oxidizing agents. Both reactions can be highly exothermic and uncontrollable.

**30. D:** Combustion of coal releases significant amounts of Hg into the atmosphere. When the Hg settles into the water, it becomes methylated and concentrates in fish, making them toxic to eat.

**31. D:** When adding, the answer should be rounded to the same number of decimal places as the measurement with the fewest decimal places. The total mass is obtained by adding up all four measurements. This yields 35.5918. Since the first and second masses are precise to only a hundredth of a gram, your answer can't be more precise than this. The number 35.5918, when rounded to two decimal places, is 35.59.

**32. C:** Vectors have a magnitude (e.g., 5 meters/second) and direction (e.g., towards north). Of the choices listed, only velocity is defined as a vector. Speed, distance, and time are all quantities that have a size but not a direction. That's why, for example, a car's speedometer reads 35 miles/hour, but does not indicate your direction of travel.

**33. C:** Displacement is a vector that indicates the change in the location of an object. Answer A would be correct if the question asked for the total distance the person walked or if the person didn't change direction. If the person turned around 180°, the displacement could be as small as 5 meters. If the person changed directions only a fraction of a degree, the displacement's magnitude would be *less* than 13 meters, not as *large* as 13 meters.

**34. C:** To add and subtract vectors algebraically, you add and subtract their components. To add vectors graphically, you shift the location of the vectors so that they are connected tip-to-tail. The resultant is a vector that starts at the tail of the first vector and ends at the tip of the second. To subtract vectors, connect the vectors tip to tail, starting with the vector that is not subtracted, and ending with the one that is. Think of this just like vector addition, except the vector that is subtracted (the one with the negative sign in front of it) switches directions.

**35. B:** The answer can be determined because the rate of acceleration is uniform. Since the acceleration is $5\ m/s^2$, the velocity increases by 5 m/s every second. If it starts at 20 m/s, it will be going 25 m/s after 1 second. After another second, it will be going 30 m/s, so the total time is 2 seconds. You can also calculate this time by using the average speed. Since the object undergoes uniform acceleration, the average speed is 25 m/s. Using the distance traveled, the same result is obtained. $t = \frac{d}{v} = \frac{50\text{ meters}}{25\text{ m/s}} = 2\text{ seconds}$.

**36. C:** This is a problem of free fall in two dimensions. A thrown ball without air resistance will only be subjected to one force, gravity. This causes a downward acceleration of exactly $9.8\ m/s^2$ on all objects, regardless of their size, speed or position. Note: since the ball was thrown directly upwards, the horizontal acceleration is $0\ m/s^2$ and the horizontal speed at all times is $0\ m/s$. Answer choice B is wrong because the force of gravity is always pointed downward and never changes direction.

**37. A:** Newton's first law (inertia) says an object in motion stays in motion, and an object at rest stays at rest, unless external forces act on them. Choice A is an excellent demonstration because it shows the ball at rest and in motion. At rest, the ball stays at rest until a force acts on it. When the ball is moving, there is no force acting on the ball in the direction of motion. Thus, the natural state of the ball is to be at rest or moving with a constant speed. Choice C is not a good demonstration because the force of friction is what makes it hard to move the heavy object. Choice B is a good demonstration of equilibrium and friction. Running a current through parallel wires (D) has nothing to do with Newton's first law.

**38. B:** The newton can be defined in terms of the fundamental units of meters, kilograms, and seconds as $N = kg \times m/s^2$, so it is not a fundamental unit. Statement II is a result of $F = ma$, Newton's second law, which is true. If $F = 0$ N, then the acceleration is $0\ m/s^2$. If the acceleration is $0\ m/s^2$, then the speed is $0\ m/s$ or a nonzero constant. This is a nonverbal statement of Newton's first law, meaning Newton's first law can be derived from his second law. Newton's second law cannot be derived from the universal law of gravity.

**39. A:** Newton's third law states that for every action there is an equal and opposite reaction. Put another way, if object A exerts a force on object B, then object B exerts a force of the same magnitude on object A in the opposite direction. Since we're considering the force of the box on the table to be the action force, the reaction force is then the force of the table on the box.

**40. D:** There will be a gravitational force of attraction between the two spheres determined by the universal constant of gravity, the distance between the spheres, and the mass of the spheres. Since both objects are affected by this force (remember, Newton's third law says the force needs to be equal and opposite), both objects will experience a slight acceleration and start moving towards each other a tiny amount (when we ignore friction). Using $F = ma$, you know that the less massive sphere will experience a larger acceleration than the more massive one.

**41. C:** The question asks how much friction is needed to start the block moving, which means you need to calculate the force of static friction. If the question had asked about the force needed to keep the object moving at a constant speed, you would calculate the force of kinetic friction. Here, the force of static friction is equal to $\mu_{\text{static}} \times N$, where $N$ is the Normal force. The normal force ($N$) on the plastic block is the weight of the block ($w = mg$) which is $10\ kg \times 9.8\ m/s^2 = 98$ newtons. The force of static friction is $0.6 \times 98\ N = 59\ N$. Answer B is the force of kinetic friction, once the block starts moving. (Note: molecular bonding and abrasion cause friction. When the surfaces are in motion, the bonding is less strong, so the coefficient of kinetic friction is less than the coefficient of static friction. Therefore, more force is required to start the box moving than to keep it moving.)

**42. B:** The weight of the masses is determined from $W = mg$. In this case, there is a force to the left/down of $20\ kg \times 9.8\ m/s^2 = 196\ N$, and a force to the right/down of $30\ kg \times 9.8\ m/s^2 = 294\ N$. The net force is 98 N to the right/down. This force is moving both masses, however, which have a total mass of 50 kg. Using $F = ma$ and solving for acceleration gives $a = \frac{98\ \text{N}}{50\ \text{kg}} = 2\ m/s^2$.

**43. B:** Using Newton's second law $F = ma$, the acceleration of all three blocks, which have a combined mass of 9 kg, is $a = \frac{25\ \text{N}}{9\ \text{kg}} = 2.78\ m/s^2$. The force pulling the rear block is $F = ma = 4\ kg \times 2.78\ m/s^2 = 11.1\ N$. Another way of thinking of this is the tension represents $\frac{4}{9}$ of the total force, since the total mass is 9 kg and the rear block has a mass of 4 kg. This must equal the tension on the rope pulling on that block. Answer C is the tension of the string connecting the 3 kg and 2 kg masses. Answer D is the tension on the rope pulling all 3 masses.

**44. C:** All three laws of motion are operating, but the third law (forces come in equal and opposite pairs) best explains the motion. The first law (inertia) is shown from the fact that the balloon doesn't move until a force acts upon it. The second law (F = ma) is shown because you can see the force and the acceleration. The force comes from the contraction of the rubber balloon. The stretched rubber exerts a force on the air inside the balloon. This causes the air to accelerate in accordance with the second law. You can't see this acceleration because the air is invisible and because it is the air inside the balloon being pushed out through the opening that the balloon is exerting a force on. However, the air being pushed out of the balloon exerts an equal and opposite force on the balloon (this is Newton's third law), which causes the balloon to accelerate in the direction it did.

**45. B:** The moment of inertia of a point mass, $m$, about any axis is given by $mR^2$, where $R$ is the distance from the axis of rotation. The moment of inertia of a solid object is calculated by imagining that the object is made up of point masses and adding the moments of inertia of the point masses. The average radius of the particles in a hollow cylinder will be $R$ (all the mass is at radius $R$). For a solid cylinder, however, much of the mass lies at radii less than $R$, meaning the overall moment of inertia will be smaller. The moment of inertia of a cylinder of thickness $R_2 - R_1$, where $R_1$ and $R_2$ are the inner and outer radii, respectively, is calculated by $\frac{1}{2}m({R_1}^2 + {R_2}^2)$. For a solid cylinder, $R_1 = 0$ meters. For a thin hollow cylinder, $R_1 = R_2$.

**46. A:** In a closed system (when you ignore outside interactions), the total momentum is constant and conserved. The total energy would also be conserved, although not the sum of the potential and kinetic energy. Some of the energy from the collision would be turned into thermal energy (heat) for example. Nor is the total velocity conserved, even though the velocity is a component of the momentum, since the momentum also depends on the mass of the cars. The impulse is a force over time that causes the momentum of a body to change. It doesn't make sense to think of impulse as conserved, since it's not necessarily constant throughout a collision.

**47. A:** A collision is considered elastic when neither object loses any kinetic energy. Since the cars latch together, this can't be the case. You could prove this by calculating the cars' kinetic energy: $KE = \frac{1}{2}mv^2$. If the railroad cars had bumpers instead of couplers, the moving car would stop and transfer all its momentum and kinetic energy to the stationary car, causing an elastic collision. In a closed system like this one, however, the conservation of momentum is an absolute law, where an object's momentum is its mass times its velocity. There are no external forces acting on the two cars. The only forces are between the two cars themselves. The momentum before the collision is the same as the momentum after the collision: $mv_{initial} + m\left(0\frac{\text{m}}{\text{s}}\right) = mv_{final} + mv_{final}$. So $mv_{initial} = 2mv_{final}$, and $v_{initial} = 2v_{final}$. Thus, the final velocity is half the initial velocity.

**48. D:** Since this is a head-on elastic collision, you could use conservation of kinetic energy and momentum to actually solve this problem. However, in this case, you only need to think through the answers to arrive at a correct conclusion. After the ball is struck, it won't be going 0 m/s. And since this is an elastic collision, and it is hit by a much larger ball, it must be going faster than the larger ball was originally moving. Therefore, the ball will be moving at more than 10 m/s. If this were an inelastic collision where the balls stuck together, the balls' final velocity would be less than 10 m/s.

**49. A:** Since the box is moving at a uniform speed, the net force on the box is 0 newtons. Thus the work (W = Fd) is also 0 joules. Answer C incorrectly assumes that 2 newtons of force are used to move the box 5 meters, and while it's true that the teacher is pulling with 2 newtons, the frictional force counteracts this. Answer D incorrectly assumes the work performed by the teacher and the work due to friction add together for a net work of 20 newtons. Answer B incorrectly uses W = F/d. The vertical forces acting on the box—gravity and the normal force—also have a net force of 0 newtons and work of 0 joules.

**50. C:** To determine how much work is done by a gravitational force, you should calculate the change in that object's gravitational potential energy. Near Earth, gravitational potential energy is given by $U = mgh$. $\Delta U$ depends only on the change in height between initial and final positions, and the work done by gravity is $W_{grav} = -\Delta U$, hence independent of path. Therefore, the work done only depends on the change in height and not on the path taken. In answer A, the work done by gravity doesn't have anything to do with friction, so this is not a good explanation. Friction is a separate force. Answer D, although true, doesn't explain why the work doesn't depend on the path.

**51. B:** The work-energy theorem can be written $W = \Delta KE$. It is derived from Newton's second law ($F = ma$) by multiplying both sides by the distance the object moves. This work is the work done by a force on an object, and not the work done by an object. Work is only done by an object if that object exerts a force on another object, causing a change in its kinetic energy or position. The work done on an object may equal its potential energy, but only if that potential energy is converted into kinetic energy. In real-life cases, some energy is converted to heat, for example, so the change in potential energy does not equal the change in kinetic energy.

**52. A:** In addition to understanding power, this problem requires you to understand unit conversions. Power is work done divided by time taken, and the work here is the average force times distance. Since the force increases evenly from 0 to 2,000 N and decreases at the same rate, the average force is 1,000 N. Keeping in mind that 20 cm = 0.2 m and 100 ms = 0.1 s, this means:

$$P = \frac{1{,}000 \text{ N} \times 0.2 \text{ m}}{0.1 \text{ s}} = 2{,}000 \text{ W} = 2 \text{ kW}$$

**53. B:** Kinetic energy is the energy of motion and is defined as $KE = \frac{1}{2}mv^2$. Using this equation, if you double the mass and the velocity of an object, you find $KE = \frac{1}{2}(2m')(2v')^2$, or 8 times the original KE; therefore, the motorcycle has 8 times as much kinetic energy as the bicycle.

**54. A:** The total energy of an isolated system is always conserved. However, the mechanical energy may not be, since some mechanical energy could be converted into radiation (light) or heat (through friction). According to Einstein's famous equation $E = mc^2$, where E is energy, m is mass, and c is the speed of light, energy can be converted into mass, and vice versa (like in nuclear reactions). This does not affect the conservation of energy law, however, since the mass is considered to have an energy equivalent. This equation does not tell anything about the mechanical energy of a particle; it just shows how much energy would be generated if the mass was converted directly into energy.

**55. D:** Answers A, B, and C all shed light on what conservative forces are but do not answer the question of why the work on an object doesn't depend on its path. Friction is a force that causes kinetic energy to be lost and where the amount of loss depends on the path taken. Work can be expressed in multiple ways, including as the sum of potentials, and all that matters is the beginning and ending position. Think of this in terms of gravity, gravitational potential energy, and the work done by gravity. In this case, $W = \Delta PE = -mg\Delta h$, where $\Delta h$ is the change in an object's height. Dividing work by the change in position shows $\Delta PE/\Delta h = -mg$. Since $-mg$ is a force, you can say $F = \Delta PE/\Delta h$, or the force equals the work, or change in potential energy, divided by its change in position; the path taken is not a factor.

**56. B:** Power is the amount of work done divided by the time it took to do the work. A kilowatt-hour is a unit of work. A 5 Kw engine running for 12 hours produces $5 \times 12 = 60$ kilowatt-hours of work. At \$0.06 per Kw-h, this is $60 \times 0.06 = \$3.60$. The other answers all arise from math mistakes.

**57. D:** The phase of a wave changes as the wave moves. When measured in radians, the phase fluctuates between 0 and 2π radians. It is this fluctuating angle that allows two identical waves to be either in or out of phase, depending on whether their sinusoidal forms are matching or not when they cross. Answers A and B are meant to emulate the wave's amplitude and wavelength, both of which are measured in units of distance (meters, for example) and not radians.

**58. D:** The jumper's weight is $9.8\text{ m/s}^2 \times 100\text{ kg} = 980$ Newtons. Insert the weight—a force—into the equation $F = kx$, where $k$ is the spring constant and $x$ is the displacement from rest of the spring. The displacement here is 5 meters. 20 meters is unnecessary information, and just a measure of how long the spring is, not how far it was displaced. $k = F/x = 980\text{ N}/5\text{ meters} = 196\text{ N/m}$.

**59. B:** The speed of a wave is the product of its wavelength and frequency. $V = \lambda f$. Here, $V = 3 \times 12 = 36\text{ m/s}$.

**60. A:** The displacement of each wave is A and -A, so the net displacement is A + (-A) = 0; the amplitude of the resulting wave would be the maximum absolute displacement, which is 0 at this point. Had the waves both been peaking, the sum would be $A + A = 2A$. If they had both been at a minimum, the sum would be $-2A$.

**61. C:** As the amplitude of the pendulum increases due to resonance, it will swing higher. However, the period of a pendulum is not connected to how high it swings. Only the length of the pendulum affects its period. The length of a pendulum will not be affected by how high it's swinging or whether it's in resonance.

**62. A:** A standing wave remains stationary, and the fixed points at both ends are the wave's nodes. Nevertheless, a standing wave with nodes at both ends of the string can have several forms. It may have one anti-node (i.e., it will arc across), two anti-nodes (this looks like a sine wave), three anti-nodes (with 1.5 sine waves), etc. However, waves with just one anti-node will have the longest wavelength and thus the smallest frequency. For a wave with one anti-node, the string will have only one-half of a wave, so 20 m represents a half-wavelength, and the full wavelength is 40 m. Using the wave equation ($v = \lambda f$) gives the correct answer. $f = \frac{v}{\lambda} = \frac{4\text{ m/s}}{40\text{ m}} = 0.1\text{ Hz}$.

**63. A:** Refraction occurs when a wave enters a new medium. The boundary between the old medium and the new medium produces a reflected wave and a refracted wave. Since the medium is different, the speed and direction of the refracted wave changes. This changes the wavelength, but the frequency remains the same. The angle of reflection depends on the angle of incidence of the wave that strikes the boundary. The angle of refraction depends partly on this angle of incidence, but also on the indices of refraction of the two substances. Although refraction is defined as a wave changing direction when it enters a new substance, a wave will not change direction if it enters this new medium exactly perpendicular to the surface.

**64. B:** When a tuning fork vibrates, it creates areas of condensation (higher pressure) and rarefaction (lower pressure) that propagate through the air because of the air's elasticity. The distance between the condensations or rarefactions is the wavelength of the sound. The amplitude of the sound is half the difference between the pressure of the condensation and the pressure of the rarefaction. Loudness and power are both logarithmic measures that depend on the amplitude, but are not directly proportional to it. For example, doubling the amplitude will not double the loudness or power; those quantities will increase just slightly.

**65. A:** Sound travels much faster through helium than through air. Generally, the speed of sound can be calculated by $v = \sqrt{k \times \frac{P}{\rho}}$, where $k$ is the heat capacity ratio for the gas (the heat capacity at constant pressure divided by the heat capacity at constant volume), $P$ is pressure, and $\rho$ is density. Since helium has a much lower density, it would have a higher speed.

**66. A:** The frequency of a sound wave directly determines its pitch. We say the pitch of 480 Hz is higher than the pitch of 440 Hz. High and low are the words we use to describe pitch. Overtones refer to the frequencies above the fundamental frequency in a musical instrument. Two singers singing the same note at the same loudness will sound different because their voices have different timbres.

**67. A:** Transcription is the process of creating an RNA strand from a DNA template. All forms of RNA—for example, mRNA, tRNA, and rRNA—are products of transcription.

**68. D:** Operons are common in prokaryotes. They are units of DNA that control the transcription of DNA and code for their own regulatory proteins as well as structural proteins.

**69. D:** Conjugation is direct transfer of plasmid DNA between bacteria through a pilus. The F plasmid contains genes that enable bacteria to produce pili and is often the DNA that is transferred between bacteria.

**70. D:** In the lysogenic cycle, viral DNA gets incorporated into the DNA of the host. A virus in this dormant stage is called a provirus. Eventually, an external cue may trigger the virus to excise itself and begin the lytic cycle.

**71. B:** In the lytic cycle, viruses use host resources to produce viral DNA and proteins in order to create new viruses. In the process, they destroy the host cell by lysing it. For this reason, actively replicating viruses are said to be in the lytic cycle.

**72. C:** Plasmids are small circular pieces of DNA found in bacteria. Plasmids are widely used in recombinant DNA technology. They are cut with restriction enzymes and DNA of interest is ligated to them. They can then easily be used to transform bacteria.

**73. D:** The ovary houses the ovules in a flower. Pollen grains fertilize ovules to create seeds, and the ovary matures into a fruit.

**74. C:** Gymnosperms reproduce by producing pollen and ovules, but they do not have flowers. Instead, their reproductive structures are cones or cone-like structures.

**75. D:** Stomata are openings on leaves that allow for gas exchange, which is essential for photosynthesis. Stomata are surrounded by guard cells, which open and close based on their turgidity.

**76. A:** The central, supporting pillar of the tree is known as heartwood. Heartwood does not function in the transport of water, and even though it is dead, it will not decay or lose strength as long as the outer layers remain intact.

**77. D:** The phloem is the pipeline through which carbohydrates are transported to the roots. It is located outside of the xylem and lives for only a short time before becoming part of the outer bark.

**78. B:** In ferns, the mature diploid plant is called a sporophyte. Sporophytes undergo meiosis to produce spores, which develop into gametophytes, which produce gametes.

**79. C:** Alternation of generations means the alternation between the diploid and haploid phases in plants.

**80. B:** Anthers contain microspore mother cells that undergo meiosis to produce microspores. Each microspore then undergoes mitosis to develop into a pollen grain, which is the male gametophyte of flowering plants.

**81. C:** In flowering plants, the anthers house the male gametophytes (which produce sperm) and the pistils house the female gametophytes (which produce eggs). Eggs and sperm are haploid. All other tissues are solely diploid.

**82. C:** Cytokinins stimulate cell division (cytokinesis) and have been found to delay senescence (aging). They are often sprayed on cut flowers and fruit to prolong their shelf life.

**83. C:** Day-neutral plants are not affected by day length in their flowering times. Rather, they respond to other environmental cues, like temperature and water.

**84. C:** Plants exchange gases with the environment through pores in their leaves called stomata. Animals exchange gases with the environment in many different ways: small animals like flatworms exchange gases through their skin; insects use tracheae; and many species use lungs.

**85. B:** Platelets are cell fragments that are involved in blood clotting. Platelets provide a surface for the blood coagulation cascade. Its final steps are the formation of fibrinogen, which, when cleaved, forms fibrin, the "skeleton" of the blood clot.

**86. A:** The large intestine's main function is the reabsorption of water into the body to form solid waste. It also allows for the absorption of vitamin K produced by microbes living inside the large intestine. Unlike the small intestine, which also reabsorbs water, the large intestine does not produce any digestive enzymes.

**87. C:** In a positive feedback loop, an action intensifies a chain of events that, in turn, intensify the conditions that caused the action beyond normal limits. Nursing stimulates lactation, which promotes nursing. Contractions during childbirth and sexual orgasm are examples of positive feedback.

**88. B:** The placenta secretes progesterone and estrogen once a pregnancy is established. The placenta secretes hCG early in pregnancy and in small doses throughout the pregnancy.

**89. C:** In oogenesis, meiosis I produces a secondary oocyte and a polar body. Both the first polar body and the secondary oocyte undergo meiosis II. The secondary oocyte divides to produce the ovum and the second polar body.

**90. B:** The gastrula is formed from the blastocyst, which contains a bilayered embryonic disc. One layer of this disc's inner cell mass further subdivides into the epiblast and the hypoblast, resulting in the three primary germ layers (endoderm, mesoderm, ectoderm).

**91. C:** In birds and reptiles, the yolk sac contains the yolk, the main source of nutrients for the embryo. In humans, the yolk sac is empty and embryos receive nutrition through the placenta. However, the yolk sac forms part of the digestive system and is where the earliest blood cells and blood vessels are formed.

**92. D:** A lineage map describes the fates of cells in the early embryo; in other words, it tells which germ layer different cells will occupy. In some small organisms such as the nematode *Caenorhabditis elegans*, all of the adult cells can be traced back to the egg. A lineage map is not a mechanism of embryo development, but rather a tool for describing it.

**93. B:** The gastrula is the first three-layered stage of the embryo, containing the ectoderm, mesoderm, and endoderm.

**94. C:** Minerals that form on the sea floor from discarded shells are most likely part of the carbonate class. Minerals that form in karst regions and evaporitic settings may also be carbonates. Examples of minerals in the carbonate class include aragonite, dolomite, calcite, and siderite.

**95. A:** The lithification process results in the formation of sedimentary rocks. During lithification, existing rock is compacted and liquid is squeezed from its pores. Eventually, the rock is cemented together, resulting in sedimentary rock.

**96. B:** Plutonic, or intrusive, rock forms deep beneath the Earth's surface and cools slowly. Volcanic, or extrusive, rock solidifies at or near the surface. Hypabyssal rock forms below the Earth's surface but not at a depth as great as plutonic rock. Detrital rock is a type of sedimentary rock.

**97. C:** Overgrazing and deforestation directly contribute to soil erosion by destroying the natural ground cover that normally prevents soil from being washed and blown away. These activities can ultimately result in desertification, which renders land unsuitable for agriculture.

**98. C:** Physical weathering of rocks can be caused by changes in temperature and pressure, as well as the freezing and thawing of water on the surfaces of rocks. Oxidation is a chemical process, not a physical one. Therefore, it is considered an example of chemical rather than physical weathering.

**99. C:** When salt water penetrates fractures in rocks and leaves behind salt crystals that cause the rock to fracture, it is considered physical rather than chemical weathering. Chemical weathering involves changes in the molecules that make up the rocks, while physical weathering occurs when external factors act on the rock without changing its chemical composition in any way.

**100. B:** Minerals (such as olivine) that are found at the top of Bowen's reaction series weather more quickly than minerals found lower in the series. This is because minerals high in the series crystallize at higher temperatures than those found lower in the series. This means they are less stable and more susceptible to weathering than rocks that crystallize at lower temperatures, such as quartz.

**101. B:** Metamorphic rock is produced when a protolith undergoes profound changes after being exposed to extreme heat and pressure. A protolith is any rock that is transformed through this process. The original rock may be sedimentary, igneous, or metamorphic. The extreme heat and pressure that serve as the catalyst for this transformation may be produced by the intrusion of magma or tectonic activity, among other factors.

**102. A:** Quartzite, marble, and slate are all examples of metamorphic rocks, while granite is one of the most common types of igneous rocks.

**103. A:** When metamorphic rock is stressed unevenly during recrystallization, it can result in foliation. Foliation is characterized by banded rock, and it occurs when certain types of minerals are reoriented during recrystallization due to uneven shortening or compression of the rock.

**104. A:** When two tectonic plates are moving laterally in opposing directions, this is called a transform boundary. When there is friction at transform boundaries and pressure builds up, it can result in shallow earthquakes (usually at a depth of less than 25 meters). California's San Andreas Fault is an example of a transform boundary.

**105. B:** It is true that the asthenosphere is hotter and more fluid than the lithosphere. The asthenosphere is a hot, ductile layer within the upper mantle upon which the lithosphere, or the uppermost mantle and Earth's crust, is situated. Heat is transferred within the asthenosphere through a process called convection, which sometimes causes movement in the tectonic plates that make up the lithosphere.

**106. D:** The most recently formed parts of the Earth's crust can be found at mid-ocean ridges. New crust forms here when magma erupts from these ridges and pushes preexisting crust horizontally towards the continental plates. Such ridges include the Mid-Atlantic Ridge and the East Pacific Rise.

**107. C:** Chemicals should not be stored routinely on bench tops. Each chemical should be stored in a location for that specific type of chemical. When in use, chemicals may be temporarily kept on bench tops, but only in the quantities that are required for that particular situation. Chemicals should be returned to an appropriate location after use.

**108. D:** A volcano occurs when a dike (a vertical fracture in the Earth's crust that fills with magma) reaches the Earth's surface and a plume (a spurt of magma) passes through it. Batholiths are large masses of igneous rock that form beneath the Earth's surface, and a sill is a horizontal fracture in the Earth's crust that fills with magma. When an oceanic plate is subducted by a continental plate, it results in the formation of mountain ranges and volcanic arcs.

**109. B:** A volcano that is thought to be dormant is expected to erupt some time again in the future, but danger is not imminent. Dormant volcanoes are expected to erupt again in the future because they still show signs of internal volcanic activity. Extinct volcanoes are not expected to erupt again because they show no signs of activity. Active volcanoes are either erupting or about to erupt.

**110. C:** The Earth's magnetic field protects it from solar wind. Solar wind is a stream of highly charged radioactive particles that emanate from the Sun, and these particles are deflected by the magnetic field. The magnetic field is shaped like a bowl that covers the side of the Earth facing the Sun. It deflects most solar particles, but some are trapped in the Van Allen belt. Particularly strong bursts of solar wind allow particles to pass through this belt into the Earth's ionosphere and upper atmosphere, creating geomagnetic storms and auroras.

**111. D:** In 1912, Alfred Wegener proposed that the continents once formed a single land mass called Pangaea, but they have since drifted apart. Theories about the Earth's magnetic fields and plate tectonics did not emerge until years later. Once they did, they helped produce evidence to support Wegener's theory.

**112. B:** The process that causes lithospheric plates to move over the surface of the mantle is called convection. The mantle rock in the lower portion of the mantle is heated by the Earth's core and slowly rises to the surface, pushing aside cooler rock that is already there. This hotter rock eventually cools and is pushed aside by hotter rock that rises from below. This cycle, called convection, creates constant movement in the mantle that contributes to the motion of the tectonic plates.

**113. D:** Water in the liquid state generally has a higher density than water in the solid state (ice). Unlike most other substances, which become progressively denser as they grow colder, water's density only increases until it reaches a maximum density around 4 °C, after which it begins to decrease as the temperature drops further.

**114. B:** The fact that water's specific heat capacity is second only to that of ammonia means that it takes more energy to increase the temperature of ammonia than it does to increase the temperature of water. Specific heat capacity refers to the amount of energy required to increase the temperature of a substance by one degree Celsius. Ammonia has the highest specific heat capacity of all substances, and the specific heat capacity of water is the second highest.

**115. C:** A triple point on a phase diagram indicates a precise temperature and pressure where a substance can simultaneously exist as a solid, a liquid, and a gas. Isothermal means constant temperature and would refer to a vertical line rather than a point. Isobaric means constant pressure and would refer to a horizontal line rather than a point. The critical point indicates a particular temperature and pressure beyond which the substance is neither a liquid nor a gas, but a supercritical fluid.

**116. C:** The main human-caused reason for "dead zones" in portions of oceans and lakes that normally host abundant aquatic life is the use of chemical fertilizers. These fertilizers, which are high in nitrogen and phosphorous, enter lakes and rivers in water runoff and become concentrated in certain areas. This concentration, called eutrophication, eventually depletes the water's oxygen levels and renders it incapable of supporting life.

**117. C:** The majority of the solar energy that reaches Earth is absorbed by the oceans, which make up 71 percent of the Earth's surface. Because of water's high specific heat capacity, oceans can absorb and store large quantities of heat, thus preventing drastic increases in the overall atmospheric temperature.

**118. A:** The majority of weather phenomena occur in the Earth's troposphere. The troposphere is the lowest layer of the atmosphere, extending from Earth's surface up to roughly 8–15 kilometers in altitude. It contains the majority of the mass of Earth's atmosphere and 99 percent of its water vapor.

**119. B:** A guyot is defined as a seamount with a flattened top. The term "seamount" refers to any undersea volcano that is more than 1,000 meters tall. Undersea troughs are called trenches, and undersea mountain chains are called mid-ocean ridges.

**120. B:** Approximately 96.5% of seawater is composed of hydrogen and oxygen. Although seawater does contain sodium, chlorine, magnesium, sulfur, and other dissolved solids, its primary components are the same substances that make up fresh water.

**121. D:** Strip mining of coal destroys landscapes, forest, and wildlife habitats. Strip mining also causes dust and noise pollution and may contaminate groundwater. Underground coal mining lowers the water table and changes the flow of groundwater and streams.

**122. C:** Deforestation causes the loss of numerous trees. Trees store carbon dioxide ($CO_2$), the leading contributor to climate change. The process of deforestation releases some of this $CO_2$ into the atmosphere, especially if the wood is burned. $CO_2$ is also discharged from the machinery that is used in the process of deforestation. Deforestation contributes to an estimated 10 percent of all greenhouse emissions. Trees also remove carbon dioxide from the atmosphere through a process called sequestering. Less trees mean less carbon dioxide is sequestered resulting in an increase of the carbon dioxide in the atmosphere.

**123. B:** While land reclamation destroys nearby habitats, it doesn't increase biodiversity. The destruction of habitats leads to a decrease in biodiversity.

**124. C:** Advantages of biomass energy include that it's renewable, carbon neutral, and abundant. A disadvantage of biomass energy include that it requires space and may be inefficient.

**125. D:** Benefits to using fossil fuels include that they are cheap and reliable and relatively safe to extract. The technology to control pollution is already developed. The most serious drawback to using fossil fuels is that their pollution contributes greatly to global warming.

**126. B:** Buckminsterfullerene molecules or buckyballs are spherical fullerene molecules with the molecular formula $C_{60}$. Graphene is a one-atom-thick sheet of carbon. Nanoparticles are particles between 1 and 100 nanometers in size. (Buckminsterfullerene particles are one example of nanoparticles, but there are many others.)

**127. A:** Currently, the greatest benefit of genetically modified crops is to the farmer, with herbicide-resistant and pest-resistant crops. This increases profits and makes farming a little easier. Currently, foods made from genetically modified crops do not show significant increases in nutrition or shelf life. One of the greatest concerns regarding foods produced from genetically modified crops is the possibility of introducing new allergens into the food supply.

**128. B:** DNA evidence is useful in criminal investigations. Once the DNA is collected, the DNA is extracted or isolated from the sample. Then the DNA is broken into fragments. After that comes DNA electrophoresis, in which the fragments are separated according to size by placing them in a gel and applying a voltage across it. After that, key genetic codes are identified with radioactive markers, and a visual profile is developed. Finally, in DNA profiling, this profile is compared to possible suspects at a crime scene.

**129. B:** Evaporation helps to remove large substances from surface water. Soils, particularly sandy soils, filter water naturally. Bacteria and other decomposers break down contaminants into simple molecules. While photosynthesis does help reduce the amount of $CO_2$ in the atmosphere, it doesn't help purify water.

**130. C:** Oxidation-reduction reactions occur inside dry cells, which are commonly called batteries. The cathode is the oxidizing agent because it accepts electrons from the anode. The anode is the reducing agent because it loses electrons.

**131. D:** Laser light is coherent, or in phase. Laser light is monochromatic, which means it's of one wavelength or frequency (color). Laser light is collimated, which means the beams are narrow and highly directional.

**132. B:** A communication GPS receiver uses trilateration by timing signals from at least four satellites in the Global Positioning System. This allows it to determine its 3D position (latitude, longitude, and altitude) while also correcting for the receiver's clock error. Trilateration determines position, speed, and elevation. Trilateration differs from triangulation in that trilateration calculations use distances, while triangulation calculations use angles.

**133. B:** Glass cleaner traditionally was a 5% ammonia solution. Recently most glass cleaners are more environmentally friendly solutions containing much less ammonia. Bleach is a solution of 3-6% sodium hypochlorite.

**134. D:** Chalk is a form of calcium carbonate, which has the molecular formula $CaCO_3$.

**135. C:** While biodegradable plastics are renewable, it is still more expensive to produce them for now.

# Practice Test #2

**1. A student is working on a science project and is going through each step of the scientific method. After the student conducts his or her first experiment and records the results of the experimental test, what should the student do next?**

a. Communicate the results.
b. Draw a conclusion.
c. Repeat the experiment.
d. Create a hypothesis.

*Refer to the following for questions 2–3:*

> *A student is conducting an experiment using a ball that is attached to the end of a string, forming a pendulum. The student pulls the ball back so that it is at an angle to its resting position. As the student releases the ball, it swings forward and backward. The student measures the time it takes the ball to make one complete period. A period is defined as the time it takes the ball to swing forward and back again to its starting position. This is repeated using different string lengths.*

**2. The student formed the following hypothesis:**

> *Lengthening the string of the pendulum will increase the time it takes the ball to make one complete period.*

**What correction would you have the student make to the hypothesis to make it follow the classical hypothesis model?**

a. Turn it into an "if/then" statement.
b. Change "will increase" to "increases."
c. Switch the order of the sentence so that the phrase about the period comes first, and the phrase about the string's length is last.
d. No corrections are needed.

**3. What would be an appropriate control variable for this experiment?**

a. The period
b. The length of the string
c. The mass of the ball
d. The color of the ball

**4. Once a hypothesis has been verified and accepted, it becomes which of the following?**

a. A fact
b. A law
c. A conclusion
d. A theory

**5. A student has collected data on the width of tree trunks and average precipitation rates for different locations. The student wants to show the relationship between these two variables. What type of graph should be used?**

a. A multi-line graph with the width measurements on the $x$-axis and precipitation rates on the $y$-axis.
b. A scatter plot with the width measurements on the $y$-axis and precipitation rates on the $x$-axis.
c. A bar graph with the width measurements on the $y$-axis and precipitation rates on the $x$ −axis.
d. A pie chart with the width of trees shown as a percentage at different precipitation rates.

**6. A student is measuring morning and afternoon temperatures for a school project using a thermal infrared gun instrument. The instrument is calibrated incorrectly and produces a cold bias of $\frac{7}{10}$ of a degree in all the temperature measurements. How should the student deal with this error?**

a. The student should recalibrate the instrument and redo the project.
b. Since it is not a major error, the student can ignore it.
c. This is a systematic error, and the student should take it into consideration when analyzing the results by increasing the temperatures $\frac{7}{10}$ of a degree.
d. This is a random error, so the student should only mention it as a potential problem in interpreting the results.

*Refer to the following for question 7:*

Your 9th grade biology class is about to take on its first animal dissection. You have already covered the procedure in detail during class, but you know that some of the students are still feeling nervous or even a little queasy.

**7. Which of the following procedures would be INCORRECT regarding dissection?**

a. The specimen should be rinsed before handling.
b. Harmful chemicals should be disposed of according to district regulations.
c. Decaying specimens are never permitted.
d. Students with open sores on their hands that cannot be covered should be excused from the dissection.

**8. After a science laboratory exercise, some solutions remain unused and are left over. What should be done with these solutions?**

a. Dispose of the solutions according to local disposal procedures.
b. Empty the solutions into the sink and rinse with warm water and soap.
c. Ensure the solutions are secured in closed containers and throw away.
d. Store the solutions in a secured, dry place for later use.

*Refer to the following for question 9:*

A chemistry experiment is performed to determine the effect of a nonvolatile solute on the boiling point of water. Three trials are performed in which 10 mg, 20 mg, and 30 mg of salt are added to 500 mL of distilled water. Each solution is heated on a hot plate, and the elevated boiling points are recorded.

**9. What is the purpose of conducting this experiment?**

a. To test a hypothesis
b. To collect data
c. To identify a control state
d. To choose variables

**10. Which of the following is needed for an experiment to be considered successful?**

a. A reasonable hypothesis
b. A well-written lab report
c. Data that others can reproduce
d. Computer-aided statistical analysis

**11. Which of the following is a characteristic of a reputable scientific journal?**

a. Peer review of the quality of research
b. Famous scientists on the editorial board
c. Use of color graphics to represent data
d. Statistical analysis of all research data

**12. Which set of scientific thinkers is related to the study of chemistry?**

a. Newton, Einstein, Feynman, and Hawking
b. Hooke, Pasteur, Watson & Crick, and Jacob & Monod
c. Ibn Hayyan, Lavoisier, Mendeleev, and Curie
d. Hutton, Darwin, Cuvier, and Wegener

**13. When students are taught science, the information needs to be:**

a. Correct, contextualized, and explained
b. Diverse, multicultural, and functional
c. Demonstrated, teacher-prepared, and manipulative
d. Theoretical, practical, and researched

**14. Which of the following is a mnemonic strategy used in teaching science?**

a. memorizing the phrase King Phillip Came Over From Greece Saturday to help remember the biological classifications: Kingdom, Phylum, Class, Order, Family, Genus, Species
b. a guided reading strategy that involves summarizing, generating questions, clarifying, and predicting
c. think, write, discuss lectures
d. student-generated experimental procedures to answer a student-generated question

**15. Broadly speaking, learning can be divided into what two categories?**

a. active and passive
b. theoretical and practical
c. hands-on and minds-on
d. inquiry-based and book-based

**16. What will happen to light waves as they hit a convex lens?**

a. They will be refracted and converge.
b. They will be refracted and diverge.
c. They will be reflected and converge.
d. They will be reflected and diverge.

**17. Substance A has a density of $5.0\ kg/m^3$ and substance B has a density of $4.0\ kg/m^3$. What is the ratio of volume A to volume B when the masses of the two substances are equal?**

a. 1.25
b. 0.80
c. 1.12
d. 0.89

**18. The air passing over an airplane's wing is considered an irrotational fluid flow. Which of the following statements correctly describes the concept of irrotational fluid flow?**

a. The fluid flows in a straight line.
b. All particles have the same velocity as they pass a particular point.
c. A tiny paddle wheel placed in the fluid will rotate.
d. The fluid does not have any rotating points, whirlpools, or eddies.

**19. A cube of aluminum is placed at the bottom of a deep ocean where the pressure is over 20 atmospheres. What happens to the density of the cube?**

a. It remains the same.
b. It decreases slightly.
c. It increases slightly.
d. It becomes zero.

**20. Which statement correctly describes the elastic limit of a metal rod?**

a. The elastic limit occurs when a deformed object will no longer return to its original shape.
b. The elastic limit occurs when the rod breaks.
c. The elastic limit occurs when the stress stops producing a strain.
d. The elastic limit assumes that the forces between molecules in a metal act like springs.

**21. Which statement best explains why water expands when it freezes?**

a. The coefficient of thermal expansion is negative.
b. The hydrogen bonding between water molecules affects how they crystallize.
c. The density of water increases linearly with temperature.
d. The internal energy of water decreases as it cools.

**22. What does it mean when someone says that electric charge is conserved?**

a. Like charges repel, and unlike charges attract.
b. The net charge of an isolated system remains constant.
c. Charges come from electrons and protons.
d. Charge can never be created or destroyed.

**23. Which of the following is the correct definition of a conductor?**

a. A metal wire in an electrical circuit.
b. A material that contains movable electric charges.
c. A material that is not a semiconductor or insulator.
d. Any device that allows electricity to flow.

**24. Which of the following statements about a solid metal sphere with a net charge is true?**

a. If the charge is positive, it will be distributed uniformly throughout the sphere.
b. The charge will be distributed uniformly at the surface of the sphere.
c. The charge will leave the sphere.
d. The electric field will be tangent to the surface of the sphere.

**25. An electron moves in a uniform electric field in the same direction as the electric field from point A to point B. Which of the following statements is true?**

a. The potential energy of the electron decreased
b. The potential energy of the electron increased
c. The potential energy of the electron remained constant
d. The potential energy of the electron was converted into kinetic energy

**26. Which of the following is true of an electric dipole?**

a. It doesn't exist in nature.
b. The charges are equal in magnitude and both are negative.
c. The charges have opposite signs and can be unequal in magnitude.
d. The charges are equal in magnitude and have opposite signs.

**27. An electric field is pointing from south to north. If a dipole is placed in the field, how will the dipole's orientation change?**

a. The positive charge will be on the northern side and the negative charge will be on the southern side.
b. The positive charge will be on the southern side and the negative charge will be on the northern side.
c. The positive charge will be on the eastern side and the negative charge will be on the western side.
d. There will be no change in the orientation.

**28. Which law says the number of electric field lines passing through an imaginary surface is proportional to the net charge inside the surface?**

a. Coulomb's law
b. Gauss's law
c. Faraday's law of induction
d. The Biot-Savart law

**29. An electron is moving in a straight line. Another particle is moving in a straight line parallel to the path of the electron but in the opposite direction. Initially the electron and particle are far apart, but get closer together. When the two particles are in the vicinity of one another, they experience an attractive magnetic force. Which of the following is a correct inference from this fact?**

a. The particle has a north pole and a south pole.
b. The particle is positively charged.
c. The particle is negatively charged.
d. The particle has either a north pole or a south pole.

**30. In the 19th century, James Clerk Maxwell calculated the speed of light in a vacuum from the proportionality constants used in electrostatics and magnetism. Which of the following relationships correctly identifies how light moves in a vacuum?**

a. High frequencies of light travel faster than low frequencies.
b. Low frequencies of light travel faster than high frequencies.
c. All frequencies of light travel at the same speed in a vacuum.
d. Light moves at infinite speed through a vacuum.

**31. Current in an electrical circuit is normally measured in amperes. Which of the following does NOT represent an alternative way of expressing current?**

a. Coulombs per second
b. Volts per ohm
c. Electrons per second
d. Watt-volts

**32. Which of the following devices changes chemical energy into electrical energy?**

a. battery
b. closed electric circuit
c. generator
d. transformer

**33. A circuit consists of a battery and a resistor. An real ammeter is used to measure the current in the circuit and is connected in series to the circuit. Which of the following is true?**

a. The current flowing in the resistor increases.
b. The current flowing in the resistor decreases.
c. The voltage drop across the resistor increases.
d. The current flowing in the resistor remains the same.

**34. A capacitor is connected in series to a battery and a resistor. After the capacitor is charged, the battery is disconnected and replaced by a battery with a greater electromotive force (emf), causing the capacitor to gain additional charge. After the capacitor has fully charged again, which of the following statements is true about the capacitance of the circuit?**

a. It has increased.
b. It has decreased.
c. It has remained the same.
d. It has become zero.

**35. When light from a single source strikes two slits, alternating bright and dark lines appear on a screen on the far side. What is the best explanation for this phenomenon?**

a. Doppler shift
b. Diffraction and interference
c. Chromatic aberration
d. Total internal reflection

**36. Which of the following is true about a diffraction grating?**

a. The more slits per inch, the greater the amount of destructive interference.
b. Blue light diffracts more than red light in a diffraction grating.
c. A diffraction grating produces maxima and minima only for monochromatic light.
d. Light passing through a diffraction grating produces a bull's-eye pattern.

**37. Which of the following statements best explains how light can be polarized?**

a. Light waves' electromagnetic fields can be oriented in a particular direction by a polarizer.
b. Photons of light can be pointed in the same direction by microscopic holes in a polarizer.
c. Light travels in a vacuum.
d. Light is a longitudinal wave.

**38. Which of the following phenomena is most closely related to the phenomenon that produces the light from lasers?**

a. radioactivity
b. phosphorescence
c. sunlight
d. blackbody radiation

**39. Which of the following statements explains what causes a rainbow?**

a. The components of sunlight strike water droplets at different angles.
b. Water molecules produce an emission spectrum when sunlight strikes them.
c. The speed of light in water depends on its wavelength.
d. There is total internal reflection for certain wavelengths of sunlight.

**40. Which of the following statements best explains the phenomenon of total internal reflection?**

a. The speed of light is at a maximum in a vacuum.
b. Light consists of bundles of energy called photons.
c. Snell's law places a limit on the angle of refraction.
d. Light consists of transverse waves.

**41. Two rays parallel to the optical axis of a concave mirror are incident upon the mirror. Where do the two rays intersect?**

a. At a point behind the mirror
b. At infinity
c. At the center of curvature
d. At the focal point

**42. An object is 20 cm in front of a thin convex lens with a focal point of 10 cm. Where is the image located?**

a. 10 cm in front of the lens
b. 20 cm in front of the lens
c. 10 cm behind the lens
d. 20 cm behind the lens

**43. Which type of aberration does NOT occur with concave spherical mirrors?**

a. Astigmatism
b. Chromatic aberration
c. Spherical aberration
d. Distortion

**44. A nucleus absorbs a neutron and undergoes a fission reaction. Which of the following statements explains why this happens?**

a. The nucleus is more stable with the additional neutron.
b. The new nucleus is unstable.
c. Energy is released.
d. The binding energy per nucleon decreases.

**45. How is light created in the core of the Sun?**

a. Convection
b. Fission reactions
c. Fusion reactions
d. Chemical reactions

**46. Which graph segments below represent constant speed?**

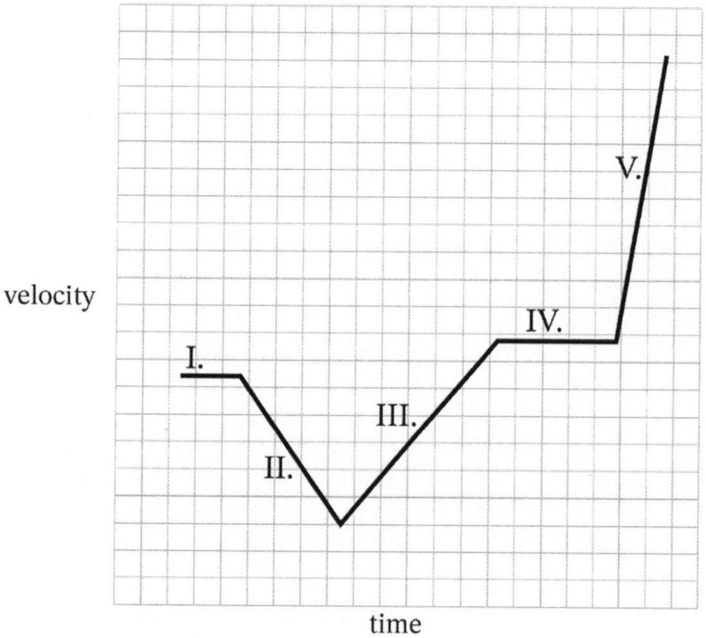


a. I and IV
b. III and V
c. II, III, and V
d. II and III

**47. Which graph segment below represents the greatest acceleration?**

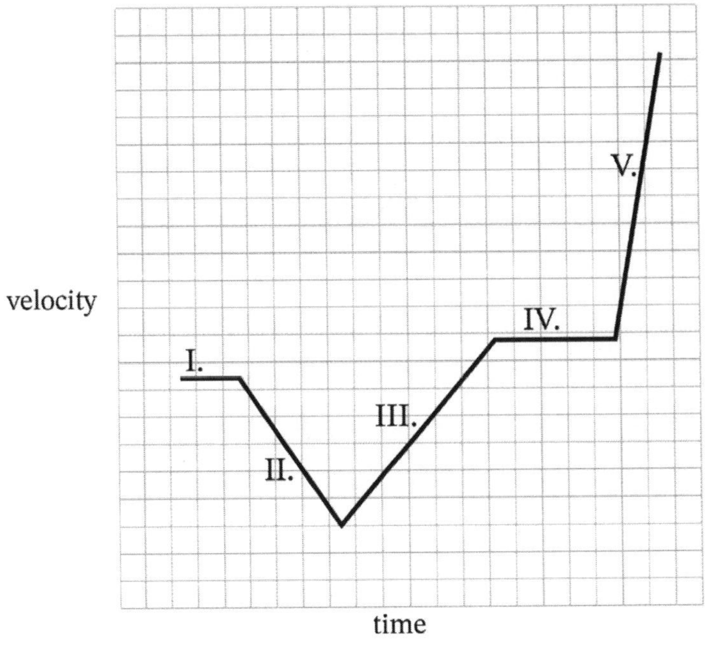


a. II
b. III
c. V
d. III and V

**48. Which of the following creates a magnetic field?**

a. The spinning and rotating of electrons in atoms
b. The separation of charged particles in atoms
c. The vibrational and translational motion of atoms
d. Loosely held valence electrons surrounding an atom

**49. Which of the following creates an electromagnet?**

a. Rapidly spinning and rotating electrons inside an iron bar
b. An iron bar moving inside a coil of wire that contains a current
c. The movement of electrons through a complete circuit
d. Convection currents within the liquid core of Earth's interior

**50. What is the scientific definition of work?**

a. The amount of energy used to accomplish a job
b. The force used to move a mass over a distance
c. The amount of energy used per unit of time
d. Energy stored in an object due to its position

**51. What property of light explains why a pencil in a glass of water appears to be bent?**

a. Reflection
b. Refraction
c. Angle of incidence = angle of reflection
d. Constructive interference

**52. Which of the following materials has randomly aligned dipoles?**

a. A non-magnetic substance
b. An electromagnet
c. A permanent magnet
d. A horseshoe magnet

**53. Which of the following equations for sound waves correctly relates frequency to wavelength and speed of sound?**

a. $f \times \lambda = v$
b. $f = \lambda \times v$
c. $f = \lambda + v$
d. $f \times \lambda \times v = 1$

**54. What characteristic of electromagnetic radiation determines if it is classified as a radio wave or an x-ray?**

a. Intensity
b. Phase angle
c. Wavelength
d. Speed of light

**55. What unit describes the loudness of a sound?**

a. Hertz (Hz)
b. Decibels (dB)
c. Meters (m)
d. Meters per second (m/s)

**56. A pulley lifts a 10-kg object 10 m into the air in 5 minutes. Using this information, you can calculate which of the following?**

a. Mechanical advantage
b. Efficiency
c. Frictional resistance
d. Power

**57. The electrolysis of water is an example of which of the following?**

a. An adiabatic process
b. A chemical change
c. A synthesis reaction
d. Reverse osmosis

**58. What type of change occurs when a liquid transitions to a gas?**

a. A phase change
b. A chemical change
c. Sublimation
d. Condensation

**59. Semiconductors belong to what group of elements?**

a. Alkaline earth metals
b. Halogens
c. Metalloids
d. Noble gases

**60. Which element will most likely form a covalently bonded compound when it bonds with sulfur?**

a. Argon (Ar)
b. Iron (Fe)
c. Lithium (Li)
d. Oxygen (O)

**61. When heat is removed from water during condensation, which of the following are formed.**

a. Atoms
b. Covalent bonds
c. Intermolecular bonds
d. Ionic bonds

**62. Which of the following would have the *most* massive radioactive decay?**

a. An alpha particle
b. A beta ray
c. Gamma rays
d. X-rays

**63. Which of the following is NOT an example of an oxidation-reduction reaction?**

a. A volcano eruption can be modeled using vinegar and baking soda.
b. Steel cans are electroplated with tin to produce grocery store food cans.
c. Blood catalyzes the decomposition of hydrogen peroxide on a cut.
d. Bread dough rises from the production of carbon dioxide gas by yeast.

**64. Which of the following conditions and chemical pairs is an example of a buffer?**

a. Homeostasis; $H_2CO_3/HCO_3^-$
b. Water has a neutral pH; $(H_3O)^+/OH^-$
c. Copper can be electroplated onto tin; $Cu^+/Sn^{2+}$
d. Aluminum hydroxide is not soluble; $Al^{3+}/OH^-$

**65. Which unit represents $\frac{1}{1000}$ of the basic metric unit of volume?**

a. Milliliter
b. Centigram
c. Kilogallon
d. Deciquart

**66. Which of the following measurements is equal to 25.4 centimeters?**

a. 10 in
b. 2.1 ft
c. 2.54 m
d. 2,540 mm

**67. In birds, gastrulation occurs along the**

a. Dorsal lip of the embryo
b. Embryonic disc
c. Primitive streak
d. Circular blastopore

**68. Which of the following does NOT obey the law of independent assortment?**

a. Two genes on opposite ends of a chromosome
b. Flower color and height in snapdragons
c. Two genes on separate chromosomes
d. Two genes next to each other on a chromosome

**69. An individual with an AB blood type needs a blood transfusion. Which of the following types could NOT be a donor?**

a. O
b. AB
c. A
d. All of the above types can be donors

**70. In humans, more than one gene contributes to the trait of hair color. What is this an example of**

a. Pleiotropy
b. Polygenic inheritance
c. Codominance
d. Linkage

**71. Which of the following ecosystems is most likely to have an inverted biomass pyramid?**

a. Forest ecosystem
b. Tundra ecosystem
c. Desert ecosystem
d. Aquatic ecosystem

*Refer to the following for question 72:*

A biome featuring scrubby plants and small evergreen trees has a hot, dry summer followed by a wetter winter. The following food chain exists in the biome:

$$tree \rightarrow caterpillar \rightarrow frog \rightarrow snake \rightarrow hawk \rightarrow vulture \rightarrow worm$$

**72. What role do vultures play in the food chain?**

a. Scavengers
b. Detritivores
c. Primary carnivores
d. Herbivores

**73. Which of the following is the major way in which carbon is released into the environment?**

a. Transpiration
b. Respiration
c. Fixation
d. Sedimentation

**74. What is the largest reservoir of nitrogen on the planet?**

a. The ocean
b. Plants
c. Soil
d. The atmosphere

**75. During primary succession, which species would most likely be a pioneer species?**

a. Lichens
b. Fir trees
c. Mosquitoes
d. Dragonflies

**76. Which of the following habitats would provide an opportunity for secondary succession?**

a. A retreating glacier
b. Burned cropland
c. A newly formed volcanic island
d. A 500-year-old forest

**77. Which biome is most likely to support the growth of epiphytes?**

a. Deserts
b. Tropical rain forests
c. Temperate deciduous forests
d. Taigas

**78. Which of the following is NOT a natural dispersal process that would lead to species colonization on an island?**

a. Mussels carried into a lake on the hull of a ship
b. Drought connecting an island to other land
c. Floating seeds
d. Animals swimming long distances

**79. When a population reaches its carrying capacity:**

a. Other populations will be forced out of the habitat.
b. Density-dependent factors no longer play a role.
c. Density-independent factors no longer play a role.
d. The population growth rate approaches zero.

**80. Which of the following is an example of a density-dependent limiting factor?**

a. Air pollution by a factory
b. The toxic effect of waste products
c. Nearby volcanic eruptions
d. Frosts

**81. Which of the following of Lamarck's evolutionary ideas turned out to be true?**

a. Natural selection
b. Organisms naturally transform into increasingly complex organisms
c. Inheritance of acquired characters
d. Body parts develop with increased usage and weaken with disuse

**82. Which of the following is a trait that results from disruptive selection?**

a. Insecticide resistance
b. Only male peacocks having colorful plumage
c. Some birds having significantly large bills than others within the same species
d. Human height

**83. Which of the following conditions would promote evolutionary change?**

a. Random mating
b. A large population
c. An isolated population
d. Gene flow

**84. Which of the following would create the greatest amount of genetic variation in a single generation?**

a. Crossing over
b. Mutation
c. Hybridization
d. Independent assortment of homologs

**85. A population of pea plants has 25% dwarf plants and 75% tall plants. The tall allele, *T* is dominant to the dwarf allele, *t*. What is the frequency of the *T* allele?**

a. 0.75
b. 0.67
c. 0.5
d. 0.25

**86. Darwin's idea that evolution occurs by the gradual accumulation of small changes can be described as:**

a. Punctuated equilibrium
b. Phyletic gradualism
c. Convergent evolution
d. Adaptive radiation

**87. The first living cells on Earth were most likely**

a. Heterotrophs
b. Autotrophs
c. Aerobic
d. Eukaryotes

**88. Evidence that humans share a common ancestor with other primates includes all of the following EXCEPT:**

a. DNA sequence
b. Fossil evidence of intermediate species
c. Analogous structures
d. Homologous structures

**89. Which of the following demographic changes would lead to a population with an older age composition?**

a. Increased birth rate
b. Environmental pollution
c. Increased availability of food
d. Medical advancements that increase life expectancy

**90. Which of the following organisms is likely to have the greatest quantity of mercury in its body?**

a. Mosquitoes
b. Frogs
c. Filter-feeding fish
d. Fish-eating birds

**91. Which of the following consequences is NOT a direct result of clear-cutting rain forests?**

a. Climate change
b. Erosion
c. Reduction in species diversity
d. Air pollution

**92. Burning fossil fuels releases sulfur dioxide and nitrogen dioxide. These pollutants lead to which environmental problem?**

a. Denitrification
b. Acid rain
c. Global climate change
d. Ozone depletion

**93. Genetic engineering:**

a. Is a form of human reproduction
b. Always involves using restriction enzymes to cut DNA
c. Always involves transient expression of genes
d. Often involves using nucleases to cut DNA

**94. Which of the following statements correctly describes a difference between surface and subsurface ocean currents?**

a. Subsurface currents are caused only by temperature variations, while surface currents are caused by changes in air pressure.
b. Subsurface currents are caused by temperature and density variations, while surface currents are caused by changes in air pressure.
c. Subsurface currents are caused by temperature and density variations, while surface currents are caused by wind.
d. Surface currents are caused by changes in air temperature, while subsurface currents are caused by changes in water temperature.

**95. The Coriolis effect in the Earth's oceans is caused by:**

a. The Earth's rotation
b. The Earth's magnetic field
c. Variations in the density of seawater
d. The Gulf Stream

**96. Which of the following statements correctly describes an effect of the Gulf Stream?**

a. It increases humidity along North America's west coast.
b. It makes the climate of South America colder.
c. It makes the climate of Northern Europe warmer.
d. It makes the climate of the Caribbean milder and less humid.

**97. Thermohaline circulation is caused by:**

a. Temperature differences between seawater only
b. Salinity differences between seawater only
c. Variations in seawater density caused by both temperature and salinity differences
d. Variations in seawater density caused by extreme wind and storm events

**98. The frequency of ocean waves is measured by:**

a. The vertical distance between a wave's crest and trough
b. The horizontal distance between the crests of two subsequent waves
c. The time between two subsequent wave crests
d. The number of wave crests that pass a given point each second

**99. When the accumulation of snow and ice exceeds ablation, which of the following occurs as a direct result?**

a. An iceberg breaks free from a glacier.
b. A glacier gradually forms.
c. A glacier slowly erodes.
d. A lake forms within a glacier.

**100. The Cretaceous-Tertiary event, during which non-avian dinosaurs became extinct, occurred approximately how long ago?**

a. 10,000 years ago
b. 15.5 million years ago
c. 38 million years ago
d. 65.5 million years ago

**101. In the field of geology, the term "uniformitarianism" refers to the belief that:**

a. Catastrophic events like mass extinctions are the main forces that have shaped the Earth.
b. The Earth's crust has not undergone any dramatic changes since its formation.
c. The natural forces that shape the Earth have remained relatively constant over geologic time.
d. The Earth's stratigraphy is more or less uniform at any given geographic location.

**102. In the field of stratigraphy, the relative ages of rocks may be determined by examining which of the following types of evidence?**

a. The dates the rocks were formed and the ages of fossils deposited within the rocks
b. Evidence of changes in detrital remanent magnetism when the rock was deposited
c. The vertical layering pattern of the rock
d. All of the above

**103. Which of the following is an example of an absolute age?**

a. A fossil is 37 million years old.
b. A rock is less than 100,000 years old.
c. An organic artifact is between 5,000 and 10,000 years old.
d. All of the above

**104. Which of the following correctly lists the periods that make up the Mesozoic era, from earliest to most recent?**

a. Jurassic, Triassic, Cretaceous
b. Permian, Triassic, Jurassic
c. Triassic, Jurassic, Cretaceous
d. Triassic, Jurassic, Permian

**105. According to the theory of evolution, which of the following life forms is thought to have appeared first on Earth?**

a. Eukaryotes
b. Arthropods
c. Prokaryotes
d. Amphibians

**106. Which of the following is considered observational evidence in support of the Big Bang Theory?**

a. Expansion in the redshifts of galaxies
b. Measurements of cosmic microwave background radiation
c. Measurements of the distribution of quasars and galaxies
d. All of the above

**107. The Cosmological Principle is best described as:**

a. An assumption that cannot be tested empirically because it has no observable implications
b. A scientific hypothesis that has been repeatedly validated in empirical tests
c. A working assumption that has testable structural consequences
d. A law of physics that defies empirical testing

**108. Redshift is observed when:**

a. A light-emitting object moves away from an observer.
b. A star begins to decrease the amount of light it emits.
c. A light-emitting object moves toward an observer.
d. A magnetic field bends observed light.

**109. Which of the following statements best describes the physical structure of the universe?**

a. Galaxies are the largest structures in the universe, and they are distributed evenly throughout space.
b. Superclusters are the largest structures in the universe, and they are distributed evenly throughout space.
c. Superclusters are the largest structures in the universe, and they are unevenly distributed so that large voids exist in space.
d. Filaments are the largest structures in the universe, and they surround large, bubble-like voids.

**110. Which of the following statements about galaxies is true?**

a. Galaxies are the only structures in the universe that do not contain dark matter.
b. Galaxies are gravitationally bound, meaning structures within the galaxy orbit around its center.
c. Galaxies typically contain over one trillion stars.
d. Galaxies are composed of clusters and superclusters.

**111. The structure of the Milky Way galaxy is best described as:**

a. Spiral
b. Starburst
c. Elliptical
d. Irregular

**112. The distance from the earth to the sun is equal to which of the following?**

a. One astronomical unit
b. One light-year
c. One parsec
d. One arcsecond

**113. The energy radiated by stars is produced by:**

a. Neutronicity
b. Nuclear fusion
c. Nuclear fission
d. Gravitational confinement

**114. The stream of charged particles that escape the Sun's gravitational pull is best described by which of the following terms?**

a. Solar wind
b. Solar flare
c. Solar radiation
d. Sunspots

**115. Which of the following planets in our solar system is NOT a gas giant?**

a. Saturn
b. Neptune
c. Venus
d. Jupiter

**116. The asteroid belt in our solar system is located between:**

a. Earth and Mars
b. Neptune and Pluto
c. Uranus and Saturn
d. Mars and Jupiter

**117. Chemical compounds are formed when:**

a. Valence electrons from atoms of two different elements are shared or transferred.
b. Valence electrons from multiple atoms of a single element are shared or transferred.
c. The nuclei of two atoms are joined together.
d. The nucleus of an atom is split.

**118. The state of matter in which atoms have the strongest bond is:**

a. Plasma
b. Liquid
c. Solid
d. Gas

**119. A calorimeter is used to measure changes in:**

a. Heat
b. Mass
c. Weight
d. Volume

**120. Commercial nuclear reactors generate electricity through the process of:**

a. Nuclear fission
b. Nuclear fusion
c. Nuclear depletion
d. Radioactive decay

**121. Which of the following diseases has been eradicated by immunization?**

a. Polio
b. Mumps
c. Measles
d. Smallpox

**122. Which of the following supplements, when taken during pregnancy, may reduce the risk of neural tube defects such as spina bifida?**

a. Vitamin B12
b. Vitamin A
c. Folic acid
d. Calcium

**123. Which of the following correctly describes the impact science has had on HIV?**

a. HIV has been eradicated by vaccinations of inactivated HIV.
b. The progression from HIV to AIDS can be controlled by antiretroviral drugs.
c. HIV can be cured by antiretroviral drugs.
d. HIV mutations have been prevented by antiretroviral drugs.

**124. Which of the following is the greatest ethical controversy related to in vitro fertilization?**

a. The fertilization outside of the mother's body
b. The multiple eggs produced by the ovary
c. The expense involved
d. The disposal of unused zygotes or embryos

**125. Which of the following is a risk in the genetic engineering of human beings?**

a. Increasing diseases
b. Limiting our genetic diversity
c. Decreasing our life span
d. Eliminating birth defects

**126. Which of the following medical imaging technologies produces detailed images using radio waves and a magnetic field?**

a. Computed tomography (CT)
b. Magnetic resonance imaging (MRI)
c. Positron emission tomography (PET)
d. Ultrasound

**127. Which of the following is true concerning the benefits of radiation therapy?**

a. Radiation therapy cannot be used to reduce pain.
b. Radiation therapy is given only to shrink tumors.
c. Radiation therapy kills only cancer cells.
d. Radiation therapy kills cancer cells by damaging their DNA.

**128. Which of the following was the first widespread use of X-rays?**

a. Medical imaging
b. Fighting cancer
c. Security scanners
d. Discovering distant galaxies

**129. Which of the following properties related to light is needed for fiber optic cables?**

a. Total internal reflection
b. Constructive interference
c. Iridescence
d. Polarization

**130. How do polarized sunglasses reduce glare?**

a. By transmitting primarily horizontally polarized light
b. By transmitting primarily vertically polarized light
c. By transmitting primarily blue light
d. By transmitting primarily yellow light

**131. When using a light microscope, how is the total magnification determined?**

a. By multiplying the ocular lens power by the objective being used
b. By looking at the objective you are using only
c. By looking at the ocular lens power only
d. By multiplying the objective you are using by two

**132. Which statement best explains the importance of recycling and using alternative sources of energy?**

a. It will lead to greater production of goods and consumer spending in the future.
b. It will benefit the health and safety of populations and the long-term sustainability of the environment.
c. It will get rid of human disease and end economic warfare in the future.
d. It will allow fossil fuel supplies to be replenished for their continued use in the future.

**133. Which of the following ethical questions regarding biotechnology would be answered and regulated by the Food and Drug Administration?**

a. Should the packaging of meat products that come from cloned animals be labeled?
b. Should nitrate or sulfate fertilizers be added to oil spills to assist the decomposition of crude oil by bacteria?
c. Should parents be allowed to genetically alter an embryo by choosing its physical characteristics?
d. Should cells or components of cells be used to create industrially useful products?

**134. What is a potential drawback that medical advances could have for human life?**

a. Medical advances require humans to constantly re-examine their moral beliefs.
b. Medical advances have drastically increased the human life span, placing stress on the environment and the economy.
c. While medical advances have cured many diseases, new diseases may still arise and threaten lives.
d. Medical advances have given people many more opportunities for treatments and drugs depending on what they can afford.

**135. Which of the following results of increased health awareness is most likely to have negative effects on society if not regulated properly?**

a. Increased funding for medical research
b. Greater health education in schools
c. Wide availability and use of prescription drugs
d. Increased knowledge of disease through worldwide awareness programs

# Answer Key and Explanations for Test #2

**1. C:** Repeating the experiment validates data. Each separate experiment is called a repetition. It should be possible to replicate the results of experiments or tests. Similar data gathered from many experiments can also be used to quantify the validity of the hypothesis. Repeating the experiments allows the student to observe variation in the results. Variation in data can be caused by a variety of errors or may be evidence against the hypothesis. Answer D, create a hypothesis, comes before experiments. Answer A, communicate the results, and B, draw a conclusion, occur after testing.

**2. A:** A formalized hypothesis written in the form of an if/then statement can then be tested. A statement may make a prediction or imply a cause/effect relationship, but that does not necessarily make it a good hypothesis. In this example, the student could rewrite the statement in the form of an if/then statement such as, "If the length of the string of the pendulum is varied, then the time it takes the ball to make one complete period changes." This hypothesis is testable, and doesn't simply make a prediction or a conclusion. The validity of the hypothesis can then be supported or disproved by experimentation and observation.

**3. C:** The mass of the ball is appropriately called a control variable for the experiment. A control or controlled variable is a factor that could be varied but that remains the same throughout all experiments for testing purposes; otherwise, it could affect the results. The length of the string is meant to be an independent variable, one that is changed during experiments to observe the results upon the dependent variable, which is the variable (or variables) that are affected. In this case, the period would be the dependent variable.

**4. D:** Once a hypothesis has been verified and accepted, it becomes a theory. A theory is a generally accepted explanation that has been highly developed and tested. A theory can explain data and be expected to predict outcomes of tests. A fact is considered to be an objective and verifiable observation, whereas a scientific theory is a greater body of accepted knowledge, principles, or relationships that might explain a fact. A law is an explanation of events for which the outcome is always the same. A conclusion is more of an opinion and could be based on observation, evidence, fact, laws, or even beliefs.

**5. B:** Scatter plots are useful for illustrating two sets of numerical data on the two axes and their relationship. In this case, by plotting the width of the tree trunks along the $y$-axis and the corresponding average precipitation rates along the $x$-axis, any relationship between the two can be found. Scatter plots are also useful when there are many data points. A multi-line graph is useful for showing sets of data that change over time. A bar graph is a good choice for comparing individual data points. A pie chart is useful for graphically comparing the parts to a whole.

**6. C:** This is a systematic error and must be treated accordingly. Answer A is probably not realistic in that the student may not be qualified to recalibrate the instrument. Answer B is incorrect, as the scientific process does not include ignoring errors and assuming they are minor. Answer D is also incorrect because it is not random and does not take into account that the collected data will be off by 0.7 degrees.

**7. C:** When performing a dissection in class, decaying specimens can be permitted under certain circumstances, but unknown specimens are never permitted. Rinsing the specimen before handling can help wash away excess preservative, which may be irritating. Disposing of harmful chemicals according to district regulations is always required. Excusing students with open sores on their hands that cannot be covered is a good precaution. Exposure to pathogens and toxic chemicals can occur through open breaks in the skin.

**8. A:** Solutions and compounds used in labs may be hazardous according to state and local regulatory agencies and should be treated with appropriate precaution. Emptying the solutions into the sink and rinsing with warm water and soap does not take into account the hazards associated with a specific solution in terms of vapors or interactions with water, soap, and waste piping systems. Ensuring the solutions are secured in closed containers and throwing them away may allow toxic chemicals into landfills and subsequently into freshwater systems. Storing the solutions in a secured, dry place for later use is incorrect, as chemicals should not be reused due to the possibility of contamination.

**9. A:** Experiments are conducted in order to test a hypothesis. Collecting data (B), identifying a control state (C), and choosing variables (D) are steps in conducting an experiment designed to test a hypothesis.

**10. C:** For an experiment to be considered successful, it must yield data that others can reproduce. A reasonable hypothesis (A) may be considered part of a well-designed experiment. A well-written lab report (B) and computer-aided statistical analysis (D) may be considered part of an experiment that is reported on by individuals with expertise.

**11. A:** A characteristic of a reputable scientific journal is that there is peer review of the quality of the research. The other choices may be characteristics of scientific journals, but these do not necessarily mean a journal is reputable.

**12. C:** Jabir Ibn Hayyan, Antoine Lavoisier, Dmitri Mendeleev, and Marie Curie are associated with the study of chemistry. Isaac Newton, Albert Einstein, Richard Feynman, and Stephen Hawking are associated with the study of physics. Robert Hooke, Louis Pasteur, James Watson & Francis Crick, and François Jacob & Jacques Monod are associated with the study of biology. James Hutton, Charles Darwin, Georges Cuvier, and Alfred Wegener are associated with the study of geology.

**13. A:** When students are taught science, the information needs to be correct, contextualized, and explained.

**14. A:** A mnemonic is a simpler, sillier, or more memorable series of words or sounds that is used to help recall a particular set of items. This strategy is often used when item order is especially important, as is the case with biological classifications. Following a guided reading strategy that involves summarizing, generating questions, clarifying, and predicting is a description of the reciprocal reading strategy. Thinking, writing, and discussing lectures are a variety of lecture styles. Following student-generated experimental procedures to answer a student-generated question is an example of an active student inquiry activity.

**15. A:** Active and passive learning are the two general categories of learning.

**16. A:** When light waves hit a convex lens, they are refracted and converge. A convex lens curves or bulges with the middle being thicker and the edges thinner. A magnifying glass is an example. Light rays are refracted by different amounts as they pass through the lens. After light rays pass through, they converge at a point called the focus. An object viewed with a magnifying glass looks bigger because the lens bends the rays inward. Choice B would indicate a concave lens as it would cause the light to be refracted and diverge. Light is not reflected in this case, so neither choice C nor D would be applicable.

**17. B:** The density of a homogeneous object, liquid, or gas is its mass divided by its volume, or the ratio of its mass to its volume. Density is inversely proportional to the volume and directly proportional to the mass. The ratio of the density of A to the density of B is $5 : 4$ or $\frac{5}{4}$. Hence, the ratio of the volume of A to the volume of B is $4 : 5$ or $\frac{4}{5}$. Alternatively, one could solve the equation $5V_A = 4V_B$.

**18. D:** Irrotational fluid flow consists of streamlines, which describe the paths taken by the fluid elements. The streamlines don't have to be straight lines because the pipe may be curved. Answer B describes the conditions for steady flow. The image of a paddle wheel may be used to explain irrotational flow, but the wheel will not turn about its own center due to vorticity. Rotational flow includes vortex motion, whirlpools, and eddies.

**19. C:** In a vacuum, the only forces acting on the molecules of aluminum are other aluminum molecules. Inside a fluid, the molecules of the fluid collide with the sides of the cube and exert a force on the surface causing the cube to shrink in size slightly. Also, the temperature of water deep in the ocean is very low. This causes the vibratory motion of the aluminum molecules to decrease, which decreases the dimensions of the cube.

**20. A:** When an external force deforms a solid material, it will return to its initial position when the force is removed. This is called elasticity and is exhibited by springs. If too much force is applied and the elastic limit is exceeded, the rod won't return to its original shape any longer. As with springs, the deformation is directly proportional to the stress. The elastic limit occurs in rods subjected to a tensile force when the strain stops being directly proportional to the stress. The typical pattern when the force increases is that the strain increases linearly, then it doesn't increase as much, and then it breaks.

**21. B:** Most substances contract when they freeze because the average distance between the atoms of the substance decreases. Water, on the other hand, forms a crystal lattice that is impacted by hydrogen bonding, and this creates gaps between the molecules when freezing. While the density of water is temperature dependent, it is not a linear relationship. While the internal energy does decrease as the water cools, this does not explain the expansion of freezing water.

**22. B:** Although like charges do repel, and unlike charges do attract, the question is indirectly asking about the law of conservation of charge. In other words, when someone mentions electric charge being conserved, they are saying the net charge of system remains constant. Charge originates from electrons and protons is only partially true because there are other elementary particles with charge. Charge can be created or destroyed because a photon will produce an electron-positron pair. There is also the example of a proton and electron combining to form a neutron.

**23. B:** Answer B correctly states the definition of a conductor. Answer C is incorrect because a current will also flow in an insulator, for example, although that current will be very low. In metals, the current flow caused by an electric field is much greater than in an insulator or semiconductor because the electrons are not bound to any particular atom, but are free to move. Answer D is incorrect because a vacuum tube is a device that electrons can flow in, but a vacuum tube is not considered a conductor.

**24. B:** In electrostatic equilibrium, excess charge on a conductor moves freely and redistributes itself so that it resides entirely on the outer surface. For a spherical conductor, symmetry causes the charge to spread uniformly over the surface, making B correct. Option A is incorrect because charge does not remain throughout the volume. Option C is incorrect because charge will not leave the sphere without a path such as grounding. Option D is incorrect because the electric field at the surface of a conductor is perpendicular, not tangent.

**25. B:** The direction of the electric field is the same as the direction of the force on a positive test charge. Moving a negative charge in the direction of the electric field requires an external force to oppose the electric field. This would increase the electron's potential energy.

**26. D:** A dipole—meaning two poles—can be either electric or magnetic and represents a pair of opposite charges with equal magnitude present in the same material. Dipoles are important in chemistry because many molecules, water for example, are polarized. The oxygen side of a water molecule has a concentration of negative charge, and the hydrogen side has a concentration of positive charge even though the molecule is neutral overall. The charges in nonpolar molecules are uniformly distributed throughout the molecule and thus they don't have any polarity.

**27. A:** Since like charges repel and opposite charges attract, putting a dipole in an electric field would cause the dipole to orient so that its negative side will point towards the electric field's positive side. Since electric fields flow from positive towards negative, an electric field pointing from south to north could be caused by positive charges in the south and negative charges in the north. Consequently, the dipole will line up opposite to this, with the positive charge on the north side. Answer B is not correct because such an orientation would be unstable. The least disturbance would cause the dipole to flip 180°.

**28. B:** This is Gauss's law, which concerns electric field lines. Electric field lines leave positive charges and enter negative charges. Electric field lines entering a surface are positive, and electric field lines leaving a surface are negative. If there is no charge inside the surface, the sum of the electric field lines is zero. Coulomb's law refers to attractive force between any two charged particles. Faraday's law regards the creation of electric fields from moving magnetic fields. The Biot-Savart law concerns the creation of magnetic fields from moving charges.

**29. B:** A moving electron produces a circular magnetic field that is perpendicular to the velocity of the particle. Since the magnetic field produced by the electron exerts a magnetic force towards the electron, the charge on the particle is positive. This conclusion requires the correct application of the right-hand rule for the creation of a magnetic field by a current (thumb in the direction of the velocity of a positive charge with fingers curling in the direction of the magnetic field) and the right-hand rule for the magnetic force on a moving charge (fingers in the direction of the positively charged particle's velocity, thumb in the direction of the magnetic force, and palm in the direction of the magnetic field). Answer D is wrong because there are no particles with only a north pole or a south pole. There may be a force between the electron and the particle if the particle is a tiny magnet, but the direction of the force would depend on the magnet's orientation, and hence answer A is wrong.

**30. C:** In a vacuum, the speed of light has nothing to do with its wavelength, frequency, or color. It's a constant $3 \times 10^8$ m/s. When light travels through a medium other than a vacuum, such as glass or a prism, it slows down, and different colors of light travel at slightly different speeds in different media. However, in most physics problems, you should treat all light as traveling at the same speed.

**31. D:** Current can be expressed as the flow of charge per time, which Answer A expresses. Answer B follows from the units in Ohm's law, V = IR. Answer C represents the number of electrons flowing per second and this corresponds to a charge flow because each electron carries the same elementary charge (so current = electrons per second × electron charge). Answer D is the only incorrect way of expressing current, although watts per volts would be an acceptable way to express amperes, which follows from the Power equation P = IV.

**32. A:** In a Zn-Cu battery, the zinc terminal has a higher concentration of electrons than the copper terminal, so there is a potential difference between the locations of the two terminals. This is a form of electrical energy brought about by the chemical interactions between the metals and the electrolyte the battery uses. Creating a circuit and causing a current to flow will transform the electrical energy into heat energy, mechanical energy, or another form of electrical energy, depending on the devices in the circuit. A generator transforms mechanical energy into electrical energy, and a transformer changes the electrical properties of a form of electrical energy.

**33. B:** Since the ammeter is connected in series, it will slightly increase the total circuit resistance, and the current in the resistor will be decreased. However, ammeters have a very small resistance so as to draw as little current as possible. That way, measuring the current doesn't significantly affect the amount of current traveling through a circuit. Voltmeters, on the other hand, are connected in parallel and have a high resistance.

**34. C:** A capacitor connected to a battery with a small internal resistance will charge up very quickly because of the high current flow. Once the potential difference on the two plates becomes equal to the emf of the battery, the electrons will stop flowing from the positive plate to the negative plate and the capacitor will be fully charged up. Connecting the capacitor to a battery with a greater emf will cause the plates to acquire a greater charge. However, the charge is directly proportional to the voltage. The capacitance is the ratio of charge to voltage and depends only on the physical characteristics of the capacitor.

**35. B:** The two slits cause the light beams to diffract, that is, spread out instead of traveling in a straight line. As a result, there are two light beams superimposed on one another. When the two light beams constructively interfere, there are bright lines, and when the two light beams destructively interfere, there are dark lines. A chromatic aberration has to do with blurring through a lens due to different colors of light. Doppler shift affects the wavelength of light from moving sources. Total internal reflection is 100% reflection of light at the boundary between certain materials.

**36. A:** Diffraction gratings produce so much destructive interference that large distances separate the bright lines due to interference. This means diffraction gratings can be used to separate light consisting of different wavelengths. Answer B is wrong because blue light, which has a shorter wavelength than red light, refracts and diffracts less than red light. The greater the wavelength of light, the more it changes direction when it hits an edge.

**37. A:** Polarization is a property of transverse waves when the medium vibrates in the direction perpendicular to the direction of propagation of energy. A polarizer orients these waves so they're all oscillating in the same direction. Polarization is a property of waves, not particles, so the particle nature of light cannot be used to polarize light. Nor are there tiny holes in a polarizer, although there are thin lines. The fact that light travels in a vacuum means that light does not need a medium, but does not affect polarization. Also, light travels in transverse, not longitudinal waves.

**38. B:** Laser is an acronym for "light amplification by stimulated emission of radiation." Lasers produce light because the substance used goes into a relatively stable excited state before emitting light. In phosphorescence, a substance absorbs light and goes into a relatively stable excited state. Light is re-emitted at a later point in time. Radioactivity produces different types of radiation from unstable nuclei. Sunlight comes from nuclear reactions in the Sun. Blackbody radiation comes from hot materials and not from the transition of atoms from a higher energy state to a lower energy state.

**39. C:** A ray of sunlight consists of many different colors of light. The speed of red light in water is slightly greater than the speed of violet light, so the angle of refraction of violet light is greater than that of red light. This causes the light to separate and creates a spectrum of colors, like in a prism. Raindrops do exhibit total internal reflection for all the wavelengths inside the droplet, although this is not what causes the rainbow. Instead, this causes a second refraction as the sunlight emerges from the water droplet, which can sometimes be seen in nature as a "double rainbow."

**40. C:** Snell's law is $n_1 \sin\theta_1 = n_2 \sin\theta_2$. This means the angle of refraction is greater than or less than the angle of incidence depending on which index of refraction is bigger. It also gives the critical angle at which there is no refracted beam. This only happens when light is in a substance with a high index of refraction and strikes a substance with a lower index of refraction at a large angle of incidence. The fact that light slows down when leaving a vacuum, coupled with the wave nature of light, leads to Snell's law. It is not relevant to understanding total internal reflection, that light is made of quanta, or that light consists of transverse electric and magnetic fields.

**41. D:** Parallel rays striking a concave mirror intersect at the focal point. If the rays weren't parallel—say they were both coming from an object near the mirror—then they would intersect elsewhere, depending on the focal length and their distance from the mirror. For example, intersecting at infinity be correct if the rays both started at the focal point. For an object between the focal point and the mirror, the virtual image is created by extending the rays geometrically behind the mirror. The center of curvature is at the center of the sphere that defines the spherical mirror and is equal to twice the focal length.

**42. D:** Since the lens is convex, the focal length is positive and the image will appear behind the lens. You can use the lens equation to solve this. $\frac{1}{f} = \frac{1}{o} + \frac{1}{i}$, where $f$ is the focal length, $i$ is the image location and $o$ is the object location. Since the object is in front it has a positive sign. $\frac{1}{10}\text{ cm} = \frac{1}{20}\text{ cm} + \frac{1}{i}$, so $\frac{1}{i} = \frac{1}{20}$ and $i = 20$ cm. The positive sign for the image means that it is behind the lens.

**43. B:** This question is asking about a concave mirror, not a lens. Since light does not pass through a mirror—it only reflects off of it—the different colors of light all bend the same amount. If light was passing through a lens, the different colors would bend slightly different amounts, causing chromatic aberration. That's not the case here. Spherical aberration occurs because the focal point of the mirror changes slightly as you move away from the center (optical axis). Astigmatism occurs when incident rays are not parallel to the optical axis. A circular beam, striking a lens or mirror at an angle to the optical axis, will become a parabola. Distortion concerns magnification and occurs in both mirrors and lenses.

**44. B:** Fission occurs when the nucleus breaks up into two smaller nuclei. When certain nuclear isotopes absorb a neutron, they become unstable and split, starting the process of fission. The average binding energy per nucleon increases with a fission reaction, and the two new nuclei are more stable than the initial nucleus. The increase in binding energy comes from the changes in mass of the protons and neutrons (note: both protons and neutrons are nucleons). The release of energy is part of the fission reaction, but this does not explain why the fission reaction occurs.

**45. C:** Sunlight consists of electromagnetic radiation in the form of photons. Sunlight is produced when hydrogen nuclei fuse to form helium. This nuclear reaction is called fusion. Fission occurs when a nucleus disintegrates into two smaller nuclei. In both fission and fusion, energy is released because the binding energy per nucleon increases. This decreases the mass of the nuclei.

**46. A:** Since change in velocity divided by change in time equals acceleration, the slope of each line segment on this graph represents acceleration. Line segments I and IV both have zero slope, meaning there is no change in velocity over the time represented. No change in velocity means the velocity is constant; therefore, lines I and IV represent constant speed.

**47. C:** All line segments on this graph represent acceleration since change in velocity divided by time equals acceleration. The line with the steepest slope represents the greatest acceleration. The steepest line is V, so option C is the correct answer.

**48. A:** A magnetic field is created by a spin magnetic dipole moment and the orbital magnetic dipole moment of the electrons in atoms. Therefore, it is the spinning and rotating of electrons in atoms that creates a magnetic field. The separation of charged particles in atoms describes the nucleus and electron clouds within an atom. The vibrational and translational motion of atoms creates thermal energy. Loosely held valence electrons surrounding an atom indicates a good electrical conductor.

**49. B:** An iron bar moving inside a coil of wire that contains a current would create an electromagnet. Rapidly spinning and rotating electrons inside an iron bar (A) creates a magnetic field. The movement of electrons through a complete circuit (C) is an electric current. Convection currents within the liquid core of Earth's interior (D) create the Earth's magnetic field.

**50. B:** Work is defined as the force used to move a mass over a distance. The amount of energy used to accomplish a job is a non-scientific definition of work. The amount of energy used per unit of time is the definition of power. Energy stored in an object due to its position is the definition of potential energy.

**51. B:** Light travels in straight lines. As light moves from one substance to another, the light rays bend according to the refractive index of each substance. As the light travels through the air, it hits the non-submerged portion of the pencil. The light is reflected from the pencil and this is what we see. However, as the light travels *into* the water, the light waves are bent (refracted), and that light is subsequently reflected and travels to our eyes. What we perceive is a pencil that is no longer whole and straight, but broken and bent. It is refraction that causes this perception.

Although the other distractors are also properties of waves, they are not the reasons why the observer perceives the pencil as bent.

**52. A:** Magnetic poles occur in pairs known as magnetic dipoles. Individual atoms can be considered magnetic dipoles due to the spin and rotation of the electrons in the atoms. When the dipoles are aligned, the material is magnetic. Choices B, C, and D are all magnetic materials. Therefore, the magnetic dipoles in these materials are not randomly aligned. Only choice A has randomly aligned dipoles.

**53. A:** The relationship between wavelength and frequency is inversely proportional, and in general, the speed of sound is constant for almost all frequencies. So, the relationship between all three is defined to be: frequency times wavelength is equal to the speed of sound in a given medium, or $f \times \lambda = v$.

**54. C:** Either wavelength or frequency can determine the classification of an electromagnetic wave (i.e., radio waves, microwaves, infrared radiation, visible light, ultraviolet radiation, x-rays, gamma rays). The intensity of an electromagnetic wave is independent from its classification. The speed of light is a constant and, as such, is what allows either wavelength or frequency to describe the wave.

**55. B:** The loudness of a sound is related to the amplitude of the wave and is measured in decibels (dB). Wave frequency is measured in hertz (Hz). Wavelength is measured in meters (m). Wave velocity is measured in meters per second (m/s).

**56. D:** The equation for power, $power = \frac{work}{time}$, can be utilized. The mass of the object (10 kg) and the distance (10 m) can be used to calculate work, $work = mass \times (gravitational\ acceleration) \times distance$. The value for time is provided.

**57. B:** The electrolysis of water is a chemical change that transforms water into hydrogen and oxygen gases. Synthesis reactions are those that combine reactants to form a product, which is the opposite of what happens when electrolyzing water. Reverse osmosis is a technique often used to purify water by forcing impure water through a semipermeable membrane using a pressure differential.

**58. A:** The addition of energy causes a phase change. Phase changes are physical changes, not chemical changes. While sublimation is an example of a phase change, it occurs when a solid turns directly into a gas without passing through the liquid state. Condensation, another phase change, occurs when a gas turns to liquid.

**59. C:** Metalloids have some properties of metals and some properties of nonmetals. Good semiconductors have the properties of metals and nonmetals, providing moderate electrical conductivity that can be regulated through temperature changes and doping.

**60. D:** Covalent bonds form when two nonmetals bond. Oxygen (O) is the only nonmetal in the answer choices. Iron (Fe) is a transition metal. Lithium (Li) is an alkali metal. Argon (Ar) is a noble gas and does not react with other elements.

**61. C:** A physical change occurs when water condenses. The only thing formed during condensation is new intermolecular bonds. Therefore, no new covalent bonds form (B). The only time new atoms form is during a nuclear reaction (A). The water molecule is not ionizing, so no new ionic bonds form (D).

**62. A:** Alpha particles are essentially helium nuclei with a mass of 4 amu. When a neutron decomposes to a proton and releases an electron, the released electron is called a beta ray (B). The mass of an electron is approximately $\frac{1}{2{,}000}$ amu. Gamma rays (C) and x-rays (D) are high-energy, short-wavelength, high-frequency electromagnetic waves. As such, they are massless.

**63. A:** A model volcano eruption using vinegar and baking soda is an acid-base reaction, not an oxidation-reduction reaction. Tin cans are steel cans with a tin coating. Applying this coating involves an oxidation-reduction reaction. Decomposition of hydrogen peroxide and dough rising through the production of CO2 by yeast are both redox reactions. Rust forming on a steel fence is a redox reaction.

**64. A:** Homeostasis involves the balancing of many biochemical systems and processes. Several of them include buffers as a means of expanding the range of stable conditions. In this instance, part of blood pH maintenance is controlled with the carbonic acid, $H_2CO_3$, and bicarbonate ion, $HCO_3^-$, buffer. While water, even when neutral, has a small amount of hydronium ions $(H_3O)^+$and hydroxide ions, $OH^-$, present, they do not act as a buffer (B). Electroplating copper onto tin is a redox reaction (C). The lack of solubility of aluminum hydroxide does not make it a buffer (D).

**65. A:** The prefix *milli-* means $\frac{1}{1,000}$ and the liter is the basic metric unit of volume. Centigram (B) is incorrect because the prefix *centi-* means $\frac{1}{100}$ and the gram is the basic metric unit of mass. Kilogallon (C) is incorrect because the prefix *kilo-* means 1,000 and the gallon is not a metric unit of volume. Deciquart (D) is incorrect because the prefix *deci-* means $\frac{1}{10}$ and the quart is not a metric unit of volume.

**66. A:** The conversion is done as follows: $(25.4 \text{ cm}) \times \left(\frac{1 \text{ in}}{2.54 \text{ cm}}\right) = 10 \text{ in}$. Choice B is arrived at by using the following incorrect formula: $(25.4 \text{ cm}) \times \left(\frac{1 \text{ ft}}{12 \text{ cm}}\right)$. Choice C is arrived at by using the following incorrect formula: $(25.4 \text{ cm}) \times \left(\frac{1 \text{ m}}{10 \text{ cm}}\right)$. Converting from centimeters to meters requires the use of the following formula: $(\text{cm}) \times \left(\frac{1 \text{ m}}{100 \text{ cm}}\right)$. Choice D is arrived at by using the following incorrect formula: $(25.4 \text{ cm}) \times \left(\frac{100 \text{ mm}}{1 \text{ cm}}\right)$. Converting from centimeters to millimeters requires the use of the following formula: $(\text{cm}) \times \left(\frac{10 \text{ mm}}{1 \text{ cm}}\right)$.

**67. C:** In birds, the invagination of gastrulation occurs along a line called the primitive streak. Cells migrate to the primitive streak, and the embryo becomes elongated.

**68. D:** Two genes next to each other (or within a specified close distance) are said to be linked. Linked genes do not follow the law of independent assortment because they are so close together that they are usually inherited together and less likely to be separated during meiosis.

**69. D:** An individual with AB blood is tolerant to both the A carbohydrate on red blood cells and the B carbohydrate as "self" and can therefore accept any of the 4 different blood types.

**70. B:** When more than one gene contributes to a trait, inheritance of that trait is said to be polygenic. This type of inheritance does not follow the rules of Mendelian genetics. Pleiotropy is the opposite, which one gene contributes to two or more unrelated traits. Codominace is a non-Mendelian inheritance where both alleles are expressed in a heterozygote individual, rather than the dominant allele being expressed and the recessive being masked. Gene linkage occurs between two genes that are located near each other on a chromosome and are usually inherited together.

**71. D:** Biomass pyramids are graphical representations of the total amount of organic matter present within an ecosystem. Most terrestrial ecosystems have the traditional pyramid presentation with the smallest point at the top. In aquatic ecosystems however, the pyramid is often inverted with the major producer within the system having a smaller biomass than the consumers above it. This is generally because the producers, often phytoplankton in these cases, produce multiple generations quickly while having shorter individual lives. These are then quickly devoured by the substantially larger mass of zooplankton.

**72. A:** Vultures eat carrion, or dead animals, so they are considered scavengers. Detritivores are heterotrophs that eat decomposing organic matter such as leaf litter. They are usually small.

**73. B:** Carbon is released in the form of $CO_2$ through respiration, burning, and decomposition.

**74. D:** Most nitrogen is in the atmosphere in the form of $N_2$. In order for it to be used by living things, it must be fixed by nitrogen-fixing bacteria. These microorganisms convert $N_2$ to ammonia, which then forms $NH_4^+$ (ammonium).

**75. A:** Pioneer species colonize vacant habitats, and the first such species in a habitat demonstrate primary succession. Succession on rock or lava often begins with lichens. Lichens need very little organic material and can erode rock into soil to provide a growth substrate for other organisms.

**76. B:** Secondary succession occurs when a habitat has been entirely or partially disturbed or destroyed by abandonment, burning, storms, etc.

**77. B:** Epiphytes are plants that grow in the canopy of trees, and the tropical rain forest has a rich canopy because of its density and extensive moisture.

**78. A:** Transportation by humans or human-associated means is not considered a natural dispersal process.

**79. D:** Within a habitat, there is a maximum number of individuals that can continue to thrive, known as the habitat's carrying capacity. When the population size approaches this number, population growth will stop.

**80. B:** Density-dependent limiting factors on population growth are factors that vary with population density. Pollution from a factory, volcanic eruptions, frosts, and fires do not vary as a function of population size. Waste products, however, increase with population density and could limit further population increases.

**81. D:** Natural selection was Darwin's idea, not Lamarck's. Mendel discovered that genes are the basic units of inheritance. Lamarck's observation about use and disuse is true, although he did not connect it with the underlying mechanism of natural selection.

**82. C:** Disruptive selection occurs when the environment favors alleles for extreme traits. In the example, seasonal changes can make different types of food available at different times of the year, favoring the large or small bills.

**83. D:** Random mating (A) or a large (B) or isolated (C) population describe conditions that would lead to genetic equilibrium, where no evolution would occur. Gene flow, which is the introduction or removal of alleles from a population, would allow natural selection to work and could promote evolutionary change.

**84. C:** Hybridization produces the greatest genetic variation in a single generation because it combines alleles from genetically distinct individuals or populations, introducing many new allele combinations at once. In contrast, crossing over and independent assortment only reshuffle existing alleles, and mutation introduces new variation more slowly, typically affecting only one or a few genes at a time.

**85. C:** According to Hardy-Weinberg equilibrium, $p + q = 1$ and $p^2 + 2pq + q^2 = 1$. In this scenario, $q^2 = 0.25$, so $q = 0.5$, and $p$ must also be 0.5.

**86. B:** Phyletic gradualism is the view that evolution occurs at a more or less constant rate. Contrary to this view, punctuated equilibrium holds that evolutionary history consists of long periods of stasis punctuated by geologically short periods of evolution. This theory predicts that there will be few fossils revealing intermediate stages of evolution, whereas phyletic gradualism views the lack of intermediate-stage fossils as a deficit in the fossil record that will resolve when enough specimens are collected.

**87. A:** The first living organisms probably had not yet evolved the ability to synthesize their own organic molecules for food. They were probably heterotrophs that consumed nutrition from the "organic soup."

**88. C:** Analogous structures do not reveal anything about common ancestors between species. They are simply features that arise due to adapting to similar ecological conditions.

**89. D:** Prolonging the life of individuals in a current population will lead to an older age composition. An increased birth rate will cause population growth, but a greater proportion will be younger, not older.

**90. D:** Mercury is a fat-soluble pollutant and can be stored in body tissues. Animals higher up the food chain, which eat other animals, are most likely to accumulate mercury in their bodies.

**91. D:** Air pollution would not be a direct result of clear-cutting forests. Air pollution would be an indirect consequence, because the $CO_2$ contained in the wood is released when the wood is either burnt or decomposed. Deforestation contributes to an estimated ten percent of all emissions. With less trees to reduce $CO_2$ already present in the air, clear-cutting results in increased atmospheric $CO_2$, as well as localized climate change. Due to deforestation roots lose strength and cause the soil to become loose, this combined with the lack of trees and shrubs to absorb water during heavy rainfall, rapid runoff occurs causing flooding and erosion. This can develop into mudslides such as the 2017 Sierra Leone mudslide disaster which resulted in the death of 1,141 people and left 3,000 homeless.

**92. B:** When sulfur dioxide and nitrogen dioxide mix with water and other substances in the atmosphere, they produce sulfuric acid and nitric acid. These acids kill plants and animals when they reach the surface of the earth.

**93. D:** *Genetic engineering* is a general term to describe altering DNA sequences through adding or removing pieces of DNA from a native sequence. In the earliest genetic engineering processes, restriction enzymes were used to perform this "clipping" function, but other methods have been devised and are in use today. Current technologies include those using nucleases (such as CRISPR-Cas9, zinc-finger nucleases, or TALENs) or site-specific recombinases.

**94. C:** It is true that subsurface currents are driven by temperature and density variations, while surface currents are driven by wind. Ocean currents affect vast quantities of seawater and strongly influence the climate of Earth's landmasses.

**95. A:** The appearance of the Coriolis effect in the Earth's oceans is caused by the Earth's rotation. The Coriolis effect results when free objects such as water move over a rotating surface such as the Earth. As water moves from the poles towards the equator, it curves slightly westward, while water moving in the opposite direction (from the equator towards the poles) moves slightly eastward.

**96. C:** The Gulf Stream, which is a surface current that originates in the Gulf of Mexico and travels across the Atlantic Ocean, makes the climate of Northern Europe warmer. After traveling up the eastern coast of the US, the Gulf Stream splits into two forks. The North Atlantic Drift travels across the ocean to warm Europe, while the southern fork travels toward West Africa.

**97. C:** Thermohaline circulation is caused by variations in seawater density caused by both temperature and salinity differences. This process, which affects subsurface ocean currents, contributes to the mixing of seawater and accounts for the relative uniformity of the water's physical and chemical properties.

**98. D:** The frequency of ocean waves is measured by the number of wave crests that pass a given point each second. The crest of a wave is its highest point, and the trough is its lowest point. The horizontal distance between two subsequent crests is called wavelength, and the height is the vertical distance between a single wave's trough and crest.

**99. B:** When the accumulation of snow and ice exceeds ablation, a glacier will gradually form. Ablation is the sloughing off of ice and snow through melting, evaporation, sublimation, and wind erosion. When snow and ice accumulate faster than ablation occurs, a glacier will form and continue to gain mass until the rate of ablation overtakes the rate of accumulation.

**100. D:** The Cretaceous-Tertiary event, during which non-avian dinosaurs became extinct, occurred approximately 65.5 million years ago. It is the most recent of the five major extinction events that have occurred throughout the Earth's history.

**101. C:** In the field of geology, the term "uniformitarianism" refers to the belief that the natural forces, laws, and processes that shape the Earth have remained relatively constant over geologic time. This belief contradicts catastrophism, which maintains that dramatic events have been the primary forces involved in shaping the Earth.

**102. D:** The field of stratigraphy is divided into several subfields, each of which focuses on a unique aspect of sedimentary material and yields unique insights about the material's age. In the subfield of chronostratigraphy, a material's age is estimated by determining when it was formed or deposited. The study of the vertical layering of rock types is called lithostratigraphy, and the study of fossil ages in rock layers is called biostratigraphy. Magnetostratigraphy examines data about changes in detrital remanent magnetism (DRM) at the time rocks were formed.

**103. A:** When a fossil is determined to be 37 million years old, this is an example of an absolute age. Absolute dating, which can be accomplished through the use of radiometric techniques, establishes precise ages for materials, while stratigraphic techniques only produce relative dates. Relative dating can establish approximate ages for rocks and fossils based on clues in the surrounding rock, but it cannot be used to determine absolute age.

**104. C:** The Mesozoic era is composed of the Triassic, Jurassic, and Cretaceous periods. It was preceded by the Paleozoic era, of which the Permian is the last period. The Triassic period ended about 200 million years ago, and was followed by the Jurassic period. The Jurassic period gave way to the Cretaceous period just under 150 million years ago.

**105. C:** Prokaryotes, or simple cells that lack a nucleus, are thought to have appeared on Earth approximately 3.8 billion years ago, according to the theory of evolution. Eukaryotes, or complex cells, are thought to have emerged 2 billion years ago, and arthropods are thought to have developed about 570 million years ago. Amphibians are thought to have emerged approximately 360 million years ago.

**106. D:** Expansion in the redshifts of galaxies, measurements of cosmic microwave background radiation, and measurements of the distribution of quasars and galaxies are all considered observational evidence in support of the Big Bang Theory. The abundance of certain "primordial elements" is also consistent with the theory.

**107. C:** The Cosmological Principle is best described as a working assumption that has testable structural consequences. The principle, which underlies existing cosmological theories, assumes that the view of the universe possessed by observers on Earth is not distorted by their observational location. The observable implications of this theory are homogeneity (the same types of observational evidence are available regardless of one's vantage point within the universe) and isotropy (the same observational evidence is available by looking in any given direction from a single vantage point).

**108. A:** Redshift is observed when a light-emitting object moves away from an observer. The observation of cosmological redshift supports the notion that the universe is expanding and the distance between Earth and distant galaxies is increasing. Redshift is an increase in the wavelength of light that appears visually as a movement toward the "red" end of the spectrum.

**109. D:** The physical structure of the universe is thought to consist of filaments (walls of superclusters, clusters, and galaxies) that surround large, bubble-like voids. Filaments are the largest structures in the universe, with some forming huge structures like the Great Wall and the Sloan Great Wall.

**110. B:** It is true that galaxies are gravitationally bound, so that structures within them orbit around the center. Galaxies do contain dark matter, and only the largest "giant" galaxies contain over one trillion stars. The smallest "dwarf" galaxies contain as few as 10 million stars. Clusters and superclusters are composed of many galaxies.

**111. A:** The structure of the Milky Way galaxy is spiral, meaning it has curved "arms" stretching out from a central point. While spiral galaxies have a flat, disc-like appearance, elliptical galaxies are more three-dimensional and appear to be roughly the same shape regardless of the viewing angle.

**112. A:** The average distance from the earth to the sun is equal to one astronomical unit (AU). An AU is equal to 93 million miles and is far smaller than a light-year or a parsec. A light-year is defined as the distance light can travel in a vacuum in one year, and is equal to roughly 63,241 AU. A parsec is the parallax of one arcsecond and is equal to $2.0626 \times 10^5$ astronomical units.

**113. B:** The energy radiated by stars is produced by nuclear fusion. This is the process whereby the nuclei of individual atoms bind together to form heavier elements and release energy outward. By the time this energy, which is created in the star's core, reaches the outer walls of the star, it exists in the form of light.

**114. A:** The stream of charged particles that escape the Sun's gravitational pull is called solar wind. Solar wind is composed primarily of protons and electrons, and these particles are deflected away from the Earth by its magnetic field. When stray particles do manage to enter the atmosphere, they cause the auroras (northern and southern lights) and geomagnetic storms that can affect power grids.

**115. C:** Venus is not a gas giant. The four gas giants are Jupiter, Saturn, Uranus, and Neptune. While these gas giants are larger than Earth and are composed mostly of gases, Venus is a terrestrial planet that is comparable in size to the Earth.

**116. D:** The asteroid belt in our solar system is located between Mars and Jupiter. The asteroid belt is populated by asteroids and dwarf planets that are distributed thinly enough that spacecraft can pass through the belt with relative ease.

**117. A:** Chemical compounds are formed when valence electrons from atoms of two different elements are shared or transferred. Valence electrons are the electrons located in the outermost shell of the atom, and they occupy the highest energy level. Atoms may form compounds by sharing valence electrons (covalent bonding) or by transferring electrons.

**118. C:** The state of matter in which atoms have the strongest bond is the solid state. Matter, which is defined as any substance that has mass and occupies space, can exist as a solid, liquid, gas, or plasma. The atoms or molecules that form solids possess the strongest bonds, while those that form plasma possess the weakest bonds.

**119. A:** A calorimeter is used to measure changes in heat. This instrument uses a thermometer to measure the amount of energy necessary to increase the temperature of water.

**120. A:** Commercial nuclear reactors generate electricity through the process of nuclear fission. The fission process is used to heat water, which in turn generates steam that is used to produce electricity. This process is controlled to ensure safety, but it does produce nuclear waste that requires the use of extensive procedures to dispose of it safely.

**121. D:** Smallpox is the only disease that has been eradicated by immunization. Progress has been made in the elimination of measles, mumps, and polio.

**122. C:** Women who are pregnant may benefit from taking multivitamins or nutritional supplements. Folic acid reduces the risk of neural tube defects such as spina bifida and facial deformities such as cleft palate. Pregnant vegetarians may benefit from vitamin B12. Vitamin A intake is actually restricted during pregnancy. Calcium supplements are taken to prevent osteoporosis.

**123. B:** Currently, there is no vaccine and no cure for HIV. HIV continues to mutate and evolve unchecked; however, the progression from HIV to AIDS can be controlled by antiretroviral drugs.

**124. D:** The disposal of unused zygotes or embryos, and even the multiple embryos lost through successive unsuccessful implants, is an issue to those who believe life begins at conception. If life begins at conception, then regulations covering experimentation on human beings should be followed.

**125. B:** Some are concerned that by genetically engineering human beings, we will greatly limit our genetic diversity. Some are concerned that only the rich or upper social class will be able to afford genetic engineering, resulting in certain traits eventually being removed from our gene pool. Potential advantages of the genetic engineering of human beings include eradicating diseases, increasing our life span, and eliminating birth defects.

**126. B:** Magnetic resonance imaging (MRI) uses radio waves and a magnetic field. Computed tomography (CT), also known as a CAT scan, uses a technique involving multiple X-rays taken from different angles. Positron emission tomography (PET) uses gamma rays emitted from radioactive isotopes. Ultrasound, also known as medical sonography, uses high-frequency sound waves.

**127. D:** Radiation therapy kills cells by damaging the DNA directly or by producing free radicals that damage the cells. Radiation therapy can kill normal cells. Radiation therapy can be used to cure cancer, prevent cancer from returning, shrink tumors, and reduce pain.

**128. A:** X-rays were put to clinical use within a month of their discovery to image bone fractures and foreign objects in the body. Later, they were used to locate tumors and to fight cancer. Distant galaxies have been discovered by the detection of X-rays from stars. X-rays are commonly used as security scanners.

**129. A:** Fiber optic cables are basically transparent strands that carry light over long distances by total internal reflection. Two conditions are necessary for total internal reflection to occur. First, the refractive index of the first medium must be greater than the refractive index of the second medium. Second, the angle of incidence must be greater than the critical angle.

**130. B:** Light from the sun vibrates and radiates out in all directions. When light is reflected from horizontal surfaces such as water or asphalt, the vibrations are aligned to be all vibrating horizontally. Polarized sunglasses have lenses that are fixed at an angle to only allow vertically polarized light to enter.

**131. A:** When using a light microscope, total magnification is determined by multiplying the ocular lens power times the objective being used. The term "ocular lens" refers to the eyepiece, which has one magnification strength, typically 10x. The objective lens also has a magnification strength, often 4x, 10x, 40x, or 100x. Using a 10x eyepiece with the 4x objective lens will give a magnification strength of 40x. Using a 10x eyepiece with the 100x objective lens will give a magnification strength of 1,000x. The shorter lens is the lesser magnification; the longer lens is the greater magnification.

**132. B:** Recycling and using alternative sources of energy reduce the amount of pollutants introduced into the ecosystem, reduce the potential for disease-related human maladies, and reduce the reliance on nonrenewable resources. Greater production of goods and consumer spending in the future would probably be good for the economy, but not necessarily the environment. Fossil fuels are considered to be a nonrenewable energy resource.

**133. A:** This is an issue that would be regulated by the Food and Drug Administration (FDA), as it regulates the packaging of meat products, among many other types of food. Answer B would not be an issue for the FDA. The Environmental Protection Agency (EPA) regulates issues regarding the environment as well as Superfund cleanups. Neither answer C, about genetic engineering of humans, nor answer D, about cell use in industry, relate to food and drugs and would not fall under the jurisdiction of the FDA.

**134. B:** A longer life span does not necessarily lead to more productive years. It also leads to a larger aged population and increases the rate of population growth. Re-examining moral beliefs is not necessarily a drawback. New diseases may arise but medical advances may aid in the cure of these diseases.

**135. C:** If not regulated properly, the illicit use of prescription drugs could have a negative effect on society. It could lead to otherwise productive and healthy people becoming dependent upon prescription drugs, either inadvertently through legitimate use, or through illegal experimentation. All other answer choices are not negative outcomes of increased health awareness.